Table of Contents

Introduction

What They Don't Want You to Know

History is not what you think. The story you've been told is a carefully edited version—one that leaves out discoveries, ruins, and entire civilizations that don't fit the script. What we call "history" is often less about what truly happened and more about what certain powers decided we were allowed to know.

For centuries, pieces of the human story have been tucked away: maps that chart coastlines before they were supposedly known, ruins older than agriculture itself, artifacts that suggest technologies far beyond what "primitive" people were thought capable of. These are the *hidden truths*—clues that refuse to bow to the official narrative.

In this book, you and I will step into the role of truth-seekers. Together, we will peel back the layers of omission, suppression, and convenient forgetfulness that have defined the history you were taught.

> *The Knowledge Filter = The invisible mechanism by which inconvenient truths are buried, and official narratives remain unchallenged.*

FORBIDDEN HISTORY

HIDDEN TRUTHS

The Untold Histories, Lost Civilizations, and Forbidden
Secrets They Never Wanted You to Discover

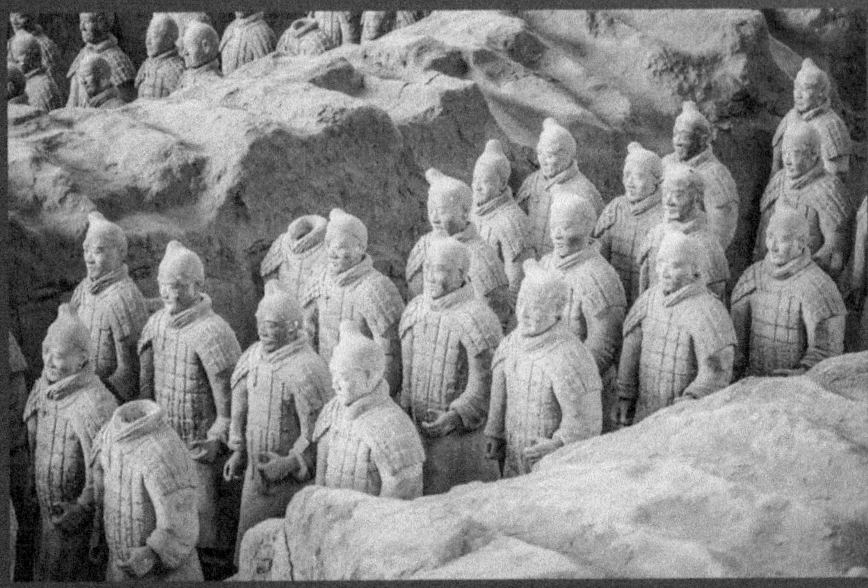

Ben Wilder

Copyright © 2025 Ben Wilder. History Publisher

Ebook ISBN: 978-1-959581-75-8

PaperBack ISBN: 978-1-959581-76-5

Legal Notice and Disclaimer

Published and Printed in The U.S.A

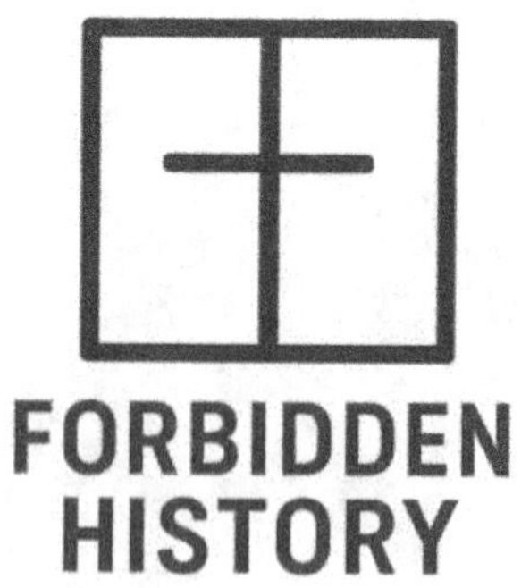

The "knowledge filter" and how information gets buried

Archaeology and history are not neutral sciences. They are governed by what I call the **knowledge filter**—a system of acceptance and exclusion that determines which discoveries make it into textbooks and which vanish into archives or private collections.

- Discover a fragment of pottery from the right century? It's celebrated.

- Uncover a tool or skeleton tens of thousands of years "too old"? It is dismissed, ridiculed, or quietly forgotten.

The **knowledge filter** ensures that only evidence supporting the established timeline is admitted. Everything else—no matter how credible, no matter how well-documented—ends up discarded.

And yet, through cracks in this filter, astonishing evidence still shines through:

- Maps from the 16th century showing Antarctica's coastline free of ice.

- Vast megalithic sanctuaries like Göbekli Tepe, predating agriculture.

- Ancient skeletons and tools millions of years old, swept under the rug by conventional science.

- Civilizations hinted at in myth—Atlantis, Mu, forgotten empires—now supported by satellite imagery and rediscovered ruins.

Why History Is Never the Full Story

The version of history you learned was built on fragile foundations. Entire chapters of our past have been erased, rewritten, or denied. Why? Because knowledge is power. Control over the story of where we came from is control over who we believe we are—and who we are allowed to become.

Civilizations rise and fall. Some vanish under oceans, deserts, or cataclysmic skies. Yet traces remain: astronomical knowledge embedded in ancient myths, massive structures aligned with the stars, and technological marvels that defy explanation.

These fragments, when assembled, suggest a truth both exhilarating and unsettling: humanity is far older, far more capable, and far more mysterious than the official record admits.

How to Use This Book: Fact, Myth, and the Middle Ground

This is not a book of myths. Nor is it blind speculation. What you will find here is an investigation into anomalies—into the cracks in the timeline. Some of what you will read is hard fact, supported by measurable data. Some reside in the twilight between fact and myth. And some, though controversial, deserve serious attention because of the patterns they reveal.

As you read, keep an open but discerning mind. Not every story is the literal truth, but within myths and anomalies often lies a core of historical reality. Our task is not to accept blindly, but to question bravely.

Approach this book as a journey: not of belief, but of inquiry. Suspend the limits of conventional history and let the evidence speak for itself.

The Journey Ahead

- **Part I** exposes cracks in the official story: underwater cities, ancient maps, and artifacts that refuse to fit.

- **Part II** explores the brilliance of forgotten knowledge—lost sciences, forbidden technologies, and wisdom preserved in myth.

- **Part III** investigates secret societies, hidden archives, and deliberate acts of suppression.

- **Part IV** connects the patterns, showing why rediscovering these hidden truths is vital to our present and future.

At the end of this book, you will find a **Workbook Bonus**—designed to help you reflect, investigate further, and form your conclusions.

Why It Matters Now

Why revisit the forbidden corners of history? Because the past is never truly past.

The ruins are real. The manuscripts exist. The evidence is waiting. If civilizations before us rose, thrived, and fell—sometimes suddenly, in fire and flood—then their stories may hold warnings and wisdom for us today.

To ignore the hidden truths is to walk blind into our future. To face them is to reclaim the real story of humanity.

So, I ask you plainly: **Are you ready to uncover the hidden truths they never wanted you to see?**

Part I: Cracks in the Official Story

Chapter 1: The Knowledge Filter

Who decides what counts as "real history"? This question is not merely academic—it cuts to the very core of our understanding of who we are. History, as most of us learned it, is not a neutral record but a carefully curated narrative shaped by institutions, gatekeepers, and paradigms that control what is admitted into the archives of "acceptable knowledge."

Universities, archaeological councils, and scientific institutions often function less like open forums of discovery and more like guardians of orthodoxy. New findings are not always celebrated; they are frequently resisted, ignored, or actively suppressed when they conflict with the reigning model of human history.

Why? Because history is power. Whoever controls the narrative of the past shapes our understanding of the present—and even our vision of the future. To challenge the official version is not simply to raise a scholarly debate; it is to threaten the very framework upon which modern civilization's identity is built.

Who Decides What Counts as "Real History"?

Behind every schoolbook, museum display, and television documentary lies an invisible council of gatekeepers: university departments, archaeological boards, funding agencies, and peer-review committees. Their collective decisions determine which discoveries enter the official record and which vanish into obscurity.

Consider the irony: a miner, farmer, or local villager may stumble upon a discovery that could revolutionize our view of human origins. But if it does not fit the accepted model, it may never be acknowledged. A single archaeologist's career can be destroyed if they present evidence of civilization older than the textbooks allow.

In the late 19th century, for example, Professor **J. D. Whitney**, California's State Geologist, reported finding advanced human tools deep within Table Mountain's gold mine shafts, sealed in strata now dated between 33 and 55 million years old. Harvard even published his findings. But William H. Holmes of the Smithsonian dismissed them, not because they were disproven, but because they contradicted Darwinian orthodoxy. Holmes wrote bluntly that if Whitney had understood the "state of human evolution," he would have kept his conclusions to himself.

Thus, the filter operates not by debunking evidence, but by forbidding its entry into history in the first place.

The Wall of Silence

The knowledge filter is enforced by multiple, subtle methods:

- **Career Threats:** Scholars who publish controversial findings risk losing tenure or grants.

- **Ridicule:** New theories are mocked as pseudoscience before being fairly evaluated.

- **Selective Funding:** Research that challenges orthodoxy rarely receives grants.

- **Textbook Control:** Even when anomalies are acknowledged, they are reduced to footnotes, stripped of their significance.

In this way, entire chapters of human history are kept from the public. What we call "history" is, in fact, a curated exhibit—carefully chosen to support a linear, comfortable narrative of progress from caveman to modern man.

Famous Cases of Ignored or Suppressed Evidence

Across the world, countless discoveries refuse to fit the official timeline. Here are some of the most striking:

1. California Gold Rush Discoveries

Miners tunneling deep into Table Mountain in the 1800s discovered mortars, pestles, spearheads, and even human skeletons encased in ancient gravels beneath lava flows. Dating shows the strata could be tens of millions of years old. Instead of prompting a re-examination of human antiquity, the evidence was filed away, boxed, and hidden in the Smithsonian's vaults.

2.   The Laetoli Footprints (Tanzania)

In 1978, scientists found footprints in hardened volcanic ash dated at 3.6 million years old. They are anatomically identical to those of modern humans. But according to official history, humans did not exist at that time. Rather than accept the implications, textbooks quietly mention them as "enigmatic."

3.   The Great Sphinx of Giza

Geological analysis reveals deep water erosion, suggesting the Sphinx endured thousands of years of rainfall long before Egypt was a desert. That would date its origins to at least 9,000 years ago—well before dynastic Egypt. Egyptologists dismiss the evidence, insisting it was built under Pharaoh Khafre around 2,500 BC.

4.   Göbekli Tepe (Turkey)

Discovered in the 1990s, this vast megalithic temple complex dates back 12,000 years, twice as old as Stonehenge. According to mainstream belief, humans at that time were still hunter-gatherers, incapable of building on such a monumental scale. Yet here it stands, rewriting history. And still, orthodox voices try to fit it into their limited models.

5. The Bosnian Pyramids

In Visoko, Bosnia, pyramid-like structures with vast tunnel systems were uncovered in the early 2000s. Evidence of advanced engineering abounds, yet mainstream archaeology has labeled them a fraud. Scholars who participate risk being blacklisted from future digs.

6. The Antikythera Mechanism

Recovered from a Greek shipwreck in 1900, this bronze device was an astronomical computer, able to track the movements of the Sun, Moon, and planets. Its complexity rivals clockwork from the 18th century, yet it is over 2,000 years old. For decades, it was dismissed as "too advanced" to be real.

7. Grooved Metallic Spheres of South Africa

Perfectly spherical objects with parallel grooves have been found in strata nearly 3 billion years old. Official science calls them "natural formations," but their symmetry suggests otherwise.

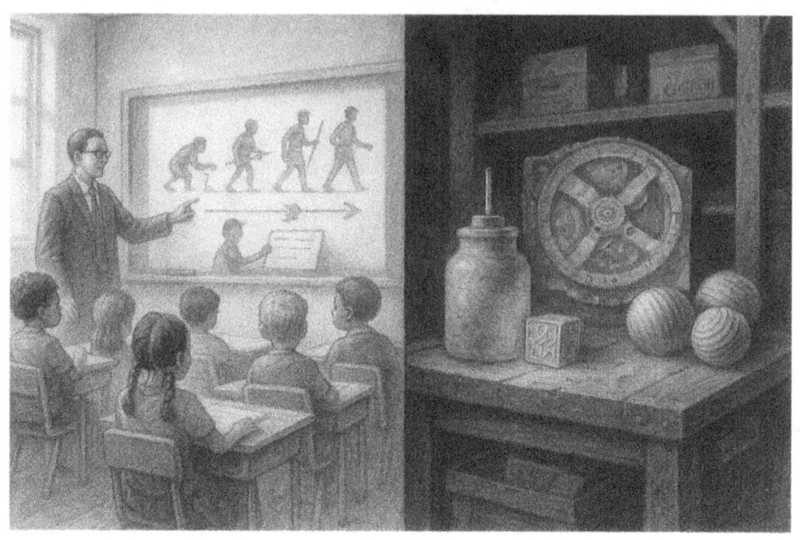

Two Versions of History: What We're Taught vs. What's Hidden

Case Study: The Baghdad Battery

Among the most intriguing pieces of forbidden archaeology is the **Baghdad Battery.**

Discovered in the 1930s near Baghdad, this unassuming clay jar contained a copper cylinder and an iron rod, sealed with asphalt. Modern reconstructions filled with acidic liquids such as vinegar generated electricity, proving the jar was a functional galvanic cell.

If authentic, the Baghdad Battery overturns our assumptions about ancient Mesopotamia. What could electricity have been used for two thousand years ago?

- **Electroplating:** Artisans may have used electricity to coat jewelry with precious metals.

- **Medical Applications:** Low-voltage electricity could have been applied in rudimentary healing practices.

- **Ritual Spectacle:** Priests may have harnessed invisible currents to impress worshippers, making idols glow or sparks leap from hidden wires.

Yet mainstream textbooks rarely mention it. When they do, it is labeled a curiosity rather than evidence of lost science. Why? Because the implications—that knowledge of electricity existed millennia before Benjamin Franklin—would force a rewrite of technological history.

Why the Knowledge Filter Persists

The filter is not sustained merely by stubbornness—it is sustained by fear. If humanity were forced to accept that advanced civilizations existed long before the textbook timeline, the consequences would be seismic:

- **Religion:** Doctrines built on linear creation stories would be shaken.

- **Science:** Entire academic careers, based on orthodox chronologies, would crumble.

- **Identity:** The belief that modern civilization is the pinnacle of progress would be shattered.

So the filter remains in place. It is easier to dismiss anomalies as errors, hoaxes, or "isolated curiosities" than to confront what they imply.

Cracks in the Wall

Yet the cracks are widening. Göbekli Tepe refuses to fit the hunter-gatherer narrative. The Antikythera mechanism now commands grudging respect. Even the Baghdad Battery is slowly reemerging in public awareness.

The knowledge filter cannot hold forever. The human spirit, restless and curious, will not remain satisfied with a sanitized version of history. The anomalies are too many, too compelling, and too insistent to ignore.

We stand at the edge of a revelation: the realization that our ancestors may not have been primitive at all, but inheritors—or survivors—of a lost epoch of advanced knowledge.

The Rising Tide of Hidden Truths

If history is a house, it was built on sand. The official version presents a linear march from savagery to civilization. But anomalies—the Baghdad Battery, Göbekli Tepe, the Sphinx, and countless others— tell a different story. A story of forgotten knowledge, suppressed truths, and civilizations erased from our textbooks.

The Baghdad Battery is not just a curiosity—it is a crack in the wall. And as more light shines through these cracks, we begin to glimpse a hidden truth: **we are not the first advanced civilization to walk this Earth.** And that realization changes everything.

Baghdad Battery: A Silent Shock to Orthodoxy

- *A clay jar with copper & iron components.*
- *Generates low-voltage current with acidic liquid.*
- *Possible uses: electroplating, healing, ritual.*
- *Official stance: dismissed as coincidence, despite experimental proof.*

Chapter 2

The Timeline Problem

How old is civilization?

Our textbooks swear humanity's "great leap" began scarcely 6,000 years ago—yet scattered clues suggest a far deeper past. Imagine a vast jigsaw whose centerpiece is missing; every new fragment we uncover refuses to fit the frame we have been told is complete. This chapter invites you to step over the velvet rope, peer behind the official exhibit, and help reassemble the picture for yourself.

Why Our Story of Civilization May Be Too Short

The modern historical calendar is a marvel of neat columns and tidy dates. It asks us to believe that after more than 190,000 years as nomadic hunter-gatherers, Homo sapiens abruptly woke up around 4000 BCE, invented writing, raised cities, and never looked back. Yet when we press gently on the edges of that timeline, the paint flakes away.

Catastrophic punctuation. A cataclysm known as the Younger Dryas—an abrupt deep-freeze that began 12,800 years ago—coincides uncannily with the first global stirrings of monumental architecture. Göbekli Tepe in Anatolia appears almost overnight, already masterfully planned. This is not the hesitant stone-piling of beginners; it is the confident hand of experience. The possibility arises that an earlier, older chapter was wiped clean by the disaster, leaving survivors to reboot culture from the ashes.

An inconvenient acceleration. Pushing farther back, anatomically modern humans have walked the Earth for roughly 200,000 years. Accepting the textbook model means tolerating 95 percent of that span in intellectual hibernation, only to sprint from tribal life to star-gazing pyramids in a few millennia. Evolution rarely works on that kind of "hurry-up" schedule. Something is missing.

The knowledge filter. When excavators hit finds that pre-date accepted horizons, the material is typically dismissed, re-dated downward, or forgotten. This unconscious sieve—what some researchers call the *knowledge filter*—silently prunes the very evidence that could rewrite history.

Consider the stone-tool layers of Hueyatlaco, Mexico. Independent geologists applied four separate dating methods—including uranium-series and fission-track—and all converged on an age *around 250,000 years.* The lead researchers expected a respectable 20,000 years, something they could publish without controversy. Instead, their careers stalled, funding vanished, and the site was closed.

> *Archaeological chronologies were constructed before scientists knew a cosmic impact devastated the planet 12,800 years ago. Any model that ignores the largest disaster since the dinosaurs is, by definition, incomplete*

If a quarter-million-year date ignites professional blowback, what else might have been swept aside—quietly, efficiently, forever?

Disputed Artifacts and Impossible Dates

Artifacts that refuse to fit the template come in every material, every epoch, every corner of the globe.

CATEGORY	EXAMPLE	REPORTED AGE	WHY IT MATTERS
Metal in stone	Grooved nickel-iron spheres from deep South-African pyrophyllite	2.8 billion years	Implies *purposeful* shaping in pre-Cambrian strata.
Human craftsmanship in coal	Gold chain pressed inside Illinois coal	300 million years	Suggests advanced metallurgy before the rise of mammals.
Anatomically modern traces	Laetoli footprints, Tanzania	3.6 million years	Identical gait and arch to present-day humans—yet the makers pre-date *Lucy* by 400,000 years.

CATEGORY	EXAMPLE	REPORTED AGE	WHY IT MATTERS
High-skill lithics	Stone blades from Hueyatlaco, Mexico	250 thousand years	Finished bifaces rival later Paleolithic craftsmanship.

Each line is a loose thread tugging at the seam of conventional chronology. Pull enough of them, and the fabric bunches, revealing a story with many more chapters than we have been allowed to read.

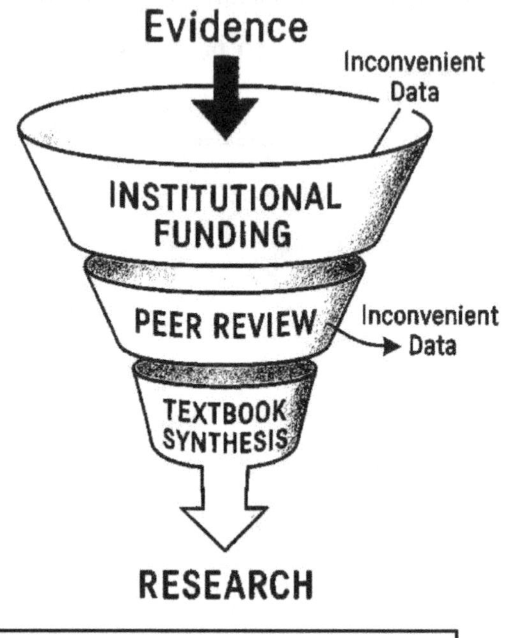

"The Evidence Pyramid"
Evidence for deep antiquity stacks upward:

1. **Context** – *undisturbed strata*
2. **Multiple dating methods** – *redundancy breeds reliability*
3. **Technological coherence** – *tools that belong to a clear chaîne opératoire*
4. **Replication** – *independent confirmations at different sites*

Dismiss any layer and the whole pyramid looks shaky; confirm them and the orthodox timeline topples.

The Mechanics of Forgetting

Why do out-of-place objects vanish from the academic conversation? Three self-reinforcing gears keep the orthodox clockwork turning:

1. **Career risk.** Publishing radical dates invites funding droughts and stalled tenure tracks.

2. **Citation amnesia.** Old reports simply go unquoted; students never learn they exist.

3. **Methodological double standards.** Contrary evidence must satisfy stricter protocols than supporting evidence.

Until those gears jam, the official story will keep recycling itself.

Case Study: The 200,000-Year-Old Tools of South Africa

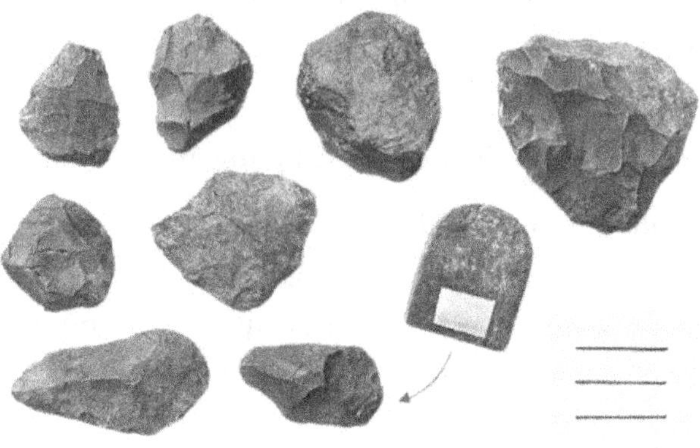

Artifacts from the Kathu Townlands, South Africa

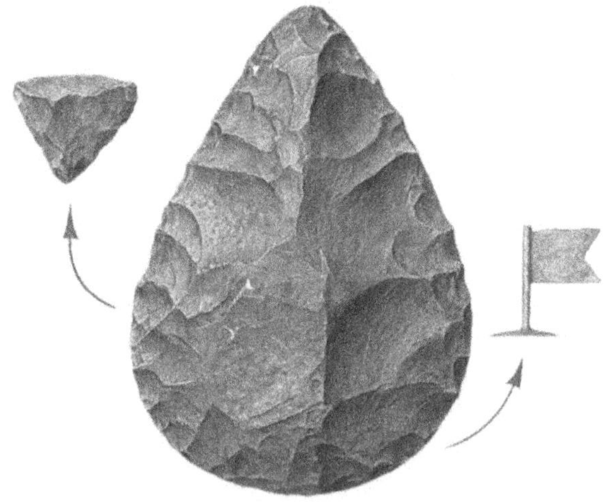

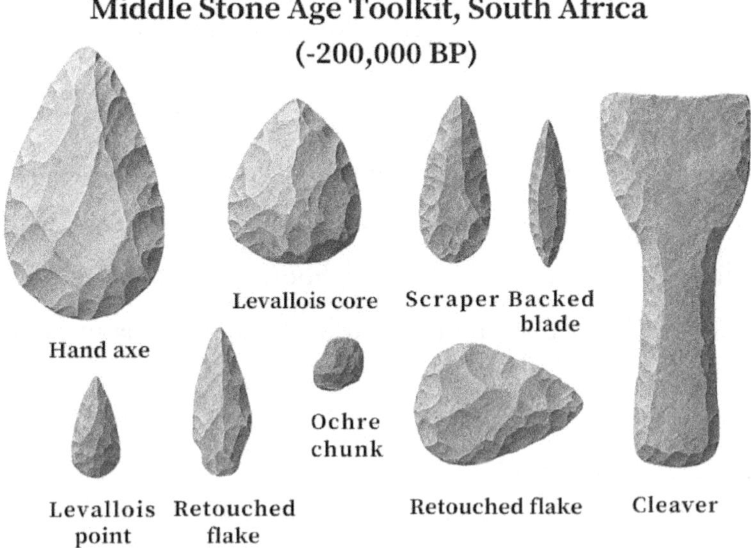

On the arid fringe between the Kalahari and the Karoo, iron-red sediments shelter a jewel box of clues. In quarries near Kathu—today a mining boomtown—archaeologists stumbled on a dense concentration of finely made stone spearheads, scrapers, and blades. Thermoluminescence and electron-spin-resonance readings cluster around **200,000 years:** the dawn of *Homo sapiens* itself.

What makes the Kathu Pan collection extraordinary?

- **Industrial-scale production.** Tens of thousands of flakes litter the horizon—a prehistoric workshop, not a sporadic campsite.

- **Blade symmetry.** Edges are straight, angles consistent, betraying a sophisticated understanding of fracture mechanics.

- **Material selection.** Artisans trekked many kilometers for cryptocrystalline quartzite prized for predictable cleavage.

These are not random "eoliths." They are precision tools, mass-produced, implying apprenticeship, planning, and social organization. Combine them with the *Klerksdorp spheres*—those hard metallic orbs with lathe-like grooves surfacing from neighboring pyrophyllite—and southern Africa morphs from footnote to headline in humanity's lost prelude.

Re-examining the Evidence

Skeptics argue the 200 ka horizon predates formal "culture." Yet the analytical checklist holds:

1. **Secure stratigraphy.** Artifact layers are sealed beneath calcrete, eliminating later intrusion.

2. **Redundant dating.** Independent laboratories converge on Middle Pleistocene ages.

3. **Technological coherence.** Core reduction sequences match later Late-Stone-Age logic, only earlier.

> **South Africa's Hidden Workshop**
> *A single square meter at Kathu Pan can yield over 900 artifacts—evidence of a manufacturing hub flourishing 200 millennia ago.*

If we grant the data its voice, the Kathu site becomes a missing paragraph in our civilizational autobiography: a paragraph hinting that advanced cognition, group learning, and large-scale planning thrived long before the reputed Neolithic spark.

Toward a New Chronology

The cumulative weight of anomalous artifacts, deep-time workshops, and abrupt post-catastrophe florescence suggests a pattern:

1. **Rise of an early, possibly global culture** >

2. **Civilizational decapitation via cosmic or terrestrial cataclysm** >

3. **Survivor knowledge enclaves** preserve fragments—astronomy, geometry, toolcraft >

4. **Re-ignition** when environmental stability returns, leaving us the half-remembered myths of "golden ages" and "bearded civilizers."

Seen through this lens, the leap from Göbekli Tepe to Sumer looks less like a miracle and more like a reboot.

Where We Go from Here

The Timeline Problem is not a puzzle to solve once and shelve; it is a running investigation. The next trench, the next core sample, the next re-examined museum drawer could upend everything—again. As you turn the page, keep an explorer's mindset: every officially "impossible" discovery is a whispered invitation to widen the story of who we are and how long we have been at the craft of civilization.

Are we pioneers at the beginning—or heirs at the tail end—of a cycle far older than our memories?

The dirt beneath our feet is answering, artifact by artifact. We merely have to listen.

Chapter 3

Lost Civilizations Beneath the Waves

Why does the ocean guard so many secrets—and what happens when those secrets begin to surface?

Imagine standing on a moon-lit promontory, the tide whispering at your feet, and realizing that the dark water beyond once nourished farms, marketplaces, and shining temples. You are not merely a spectator: you are the next witness in a detective story twelve thousand years in the making. This chapter invites you to wade in—boots, flippers, or submarine hatch—and decide for yourself which ruins are fact, which are fantasy, and which refuse easy classification.

Submerged Ruins & Drowned Cities

Human settlements hug coasts because coasts feed, connect, and inspire—but they are also the first to drown when sea levels rise. During the last Ice Age, so much water was locked inside continental glaciers that global sea level sat roughly **120 meters lower** than it does today. Between about 19,000 and 6,000 BCE, two pulses of meltwater swallowed more than nine million square miles of land. Whole cultures were erased—except where stonework, mud-brick outlines, or myths endured.

Site	Approx. Depth/Distance	Cultural Horizon	Key Finds
Pavlopetri, Greece	3–4 m, 200 m offshore	c. 3500 BCE	Streets lay at right angles, megaron houses, courtyards, ceramic kilns
Atlit-Yam, Israel	8–12 m	c. 6900 BCE	Oval houses, a semicircle of megaliths around a freshwater spring, a tuberculosis skeleton with the earliest known *Mycobacterium* DNA
Heracleion & Canopus, Egypt	6–9 m in the Nile Delta	c. 7th century B CE– 8th century CE	6-ton red-granite statues, massive quay blocks, gold coins minted on site
Dwarka, India	5–36 m in the Gulf of Khambhat	possibly 2000 – 1500 BCE	Basalt causeways, semicircular wall, and silicified wood dated to the late Holocene
Mahabalip uram "Pagodas," India	inter-tidal to 8 m	Medieval Pallava dynasty & older	Granite shrines revealed after the 2004 tsunami; sculpted elephants
Yonaguni "Monume nt," Japan	5–25 m	contested	Step-edged terraces, 90-degree angles, natural bedding planes, or quarry?

Site	Approx. Depth/Distance	Cultural Horizon	Key Finds
Cuba Deep Plateau	600–760 m	highly contested	Sonar grids resembling streets; no physical relics yet recovered

Even well-documented sites such as Pavlopetri risk vanishing a second time beneath modern anchors and rogue storms. Underwater archaeologists race not only against depth and darkness but against trawler nets that can shred a 5,000-year-old wall in minutes.

Atlantis, Doggerland & India's Sunken Temples

Atlantis—Mythic Mirror or Shattered Memory?

Plato's dialogues situate Atlantis "beyond the Pillars of Heracles," destroyed in a single day and night of floods and quakes circa 9600 BCE. Critics dismiss the story as an allegory; proponents counter that the Younger Dryas meltdown offers a credible cataclysmic backdrop. Modern surveys have eliminated many candidate regions, yet some intriguing possibilities remain:

- **Azores–Gibraltar Ridge:** volcanic plateau exhibiting Ice-Age shorelines 80–100 m below present; micro-seismic instability fits Plato's quake narrative.

- **Doñana Marshes, SW Spain:** buried estuarine rings visible on LiDAR; pottery and copper artifacts suggest Bronze Age, not Pleistocene, occupation—perhaps an *echo*, not the original.

Doggerland—Europe's Atlantis

Beneath the churning North Sea lies a once-verdant plain that connected Britain to the Continent. Core samples and oil-rig sonars have traced estuaries, elk herds, and Mesolithic hearths dated between 10,000 and 6,200 BCE. The final blow arrived when the Storegga undersea landslide unleashed a tsunami up to 20 meters high.

Artifacts so far: red-deer antler harpoons, a carved amber amulet, and pollen spectra mapping birch–pine forests. Computer reconstructions reveal lagoons where seals hauled out under summer suns, in nearly the same latitude where oil platforms now glow at night.

Meltwater Pulse 1A

• *When: c. 14,600 BCE*
• *Rise: ≈ 20 m in < 500 years*
The fastest recorded natural sea level jump; coastal societies would have faced, in human terms, overnight inundation.

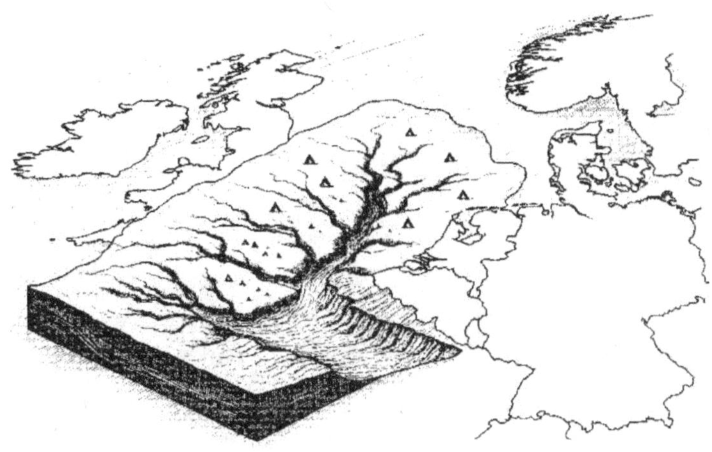

Doggerland Exposed — a cut-away bathymetric view revealing its lost river valleys, Mesolithic camp sites, and the modern North Sea coast ghosted above.

India's Drowned Sanctuaries

India preserves some of the world's longest continuous maritime texts, many reciting cities claimed by the sea. Three standouts:

- **Dwarka, Gujarat:** Sonar grids map wharves aligned to paleocoastal currents; carbon-dated wood scatters from 2280 ± 120 BCE to 1500 BCE. Coral encrustation suggests the

How to Read a Submerged Legend

1. Identify time-anchoring details in the oldest version of the tale.
2. Match those details to paleoclimate events, not modern coastlines.
3. Check for independent traditions that cross-validate the same horizon.

stone was quarried onshore, shaped, then lost as the shoreline retreated.

- **Poompuhar, Tamil Nadu:** Offshore trenches reveal brick-lined drains, semiprecious stone beads, and Black-and-Red ware pottery. Classical Sangam poetry mourns its drowning.

- **Mahabalipuram, Tamil Nadu:** Local lore spoke of "seven pagodas"; only one stood onshore until the 2004 tsunami exposed two more shrines and lion statues exactly where divers had reported "odd masonry" years before.

These corroborations between oral lore and sonar map make India a testing ground for how memory can out-swim millennia.

Science vs. Speculation—From Sonar to Storyboard

Toolbox of the Subaquatic Sleuth

Checklist for Evaluating Underwater Civilization Claims

A. Is masonry clearly quarried or tool-shaped?
B. Do finds appear in primary context (undisturbed strata)?
C. Has multiple dating technique agreement been achieved?
D. Are cultural artifacts—a shard, a carving, even a fishhook—present?.
E. Is the interpretation peer-reviewed or mainly press-released

Technique	Strength	Pitfall
Side-scan & multibeam sonar	Maps large areas swiftly in 3D	Rectilinear geology can mimic walls
Sub-bottom profiling	Detects buried layers & foundations	Saltwater reduces depth penetration
ROV & AUV imaging	Close-up verification without divers	Costs restrict time on target
Radiocarbon, OSL, U/Th dating	Anchors structures in time	Requires organic inclusions or light-sensitive grains
Paleo-botany & micro-fauna	Reconstructs vanished landscapes	Easily displaced by currents

Case Studies in Caution

- **Bimini Road (Bahamas):** Joints match natural beach-rock fracture; yet, quarry-like marks on some blocks keep debate alive.

- **Yonaguni, Japan:** Photogrammetry shows right angles correspond to natural sandstone bedding; tool-marks remain inconclusive.

- **Cuba Deep Plateau:** Until ROVs retrieve datable material, sonar-only "pyramids" remain tantalizing but unproven.

Skepticism, however, must cut both ways. Declaring every odd shape "natural" without on-site sampling can stall discovery as surely as wishful thinking can mislabel basalt cliffs as citadels.

The Quiet Revolution: Citizen Bathymetry

Kayak-mounted echo-sounders, low-cost magnetometers, and open-source seabed software now allow coastal communities to chart shallows once ignored by big research budgets. Grassroots teams have already expanded Peruvian maritime maps and located shipwrecks around Cornwall. When amateur data flags an anomaly, professional crews can target resources with surgical precision, democratizing the frontier.

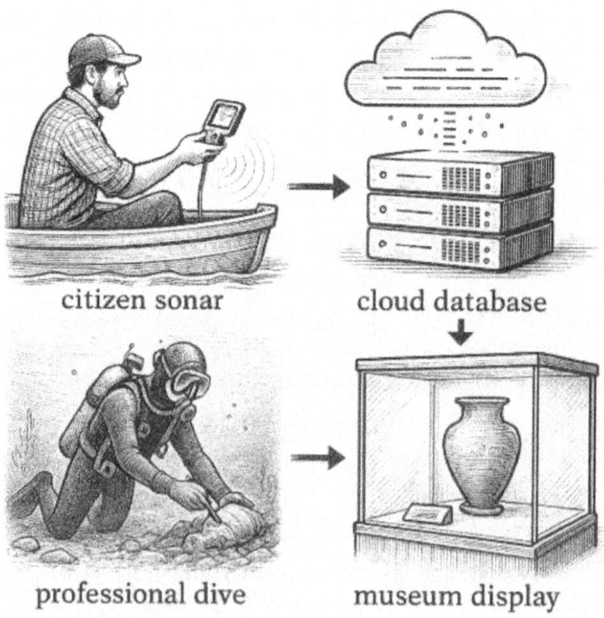

From sonar ping to spotlight: tracking an artifact's journey from citizen discovery to museum display

The Living Seafloor—Why Forgotten Civilizations Matter Today

Coastal cities house nearly *three billion* people. Understanding ancient flood narratives refines our models for future sea-level scenarios. Moreover, submerged heritage can kindle regional pride and eco-tourism, turning ghost cities into living classrooms.

Lesson	Modern Application
Rapid sea-level rise can unfold within two human lifetimes	Policy for climate migration & resilient architecture
Tsunami traces in Doggerland data.	Early-warning sensors on continental shelves
Mixed natural-cultural geology (Yonaguni, Bimini)	Training algorithms to distinguish archaeological noise in satellite bathymetry

Charting the Uncharted: A Reader's Field Manual

1. **Start Local:** Map your nearest continental shelf on public bathymetric portals; note paleoriver outlets.

2. **Cross-Check Myth & Map:** Align indigenous flood stories against deglaciation curves.

3. **Volunteer:** Many universities welcome remote analysts to tag sonar "slices."

4. **Think Multi-Layer:** A single anomaly becomes persuasive only when architecture, artifacts, and dates intersect.

5. **Stay Humble:** The ocean teaches in whispers, not manifestos.

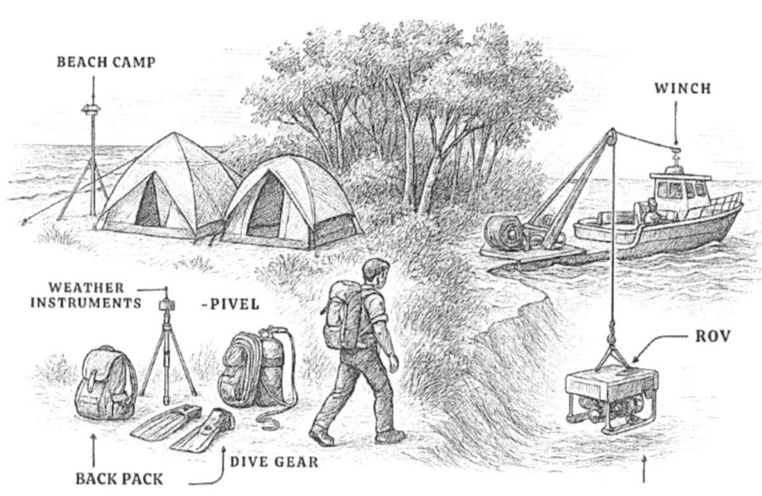

We began this journey ankle-deep in courage and chest-deep in questions. We discovered that cities do not merely sink—they migrate into story, then await retrieval by sonar, spade, and imagination. Some claims dissolve under scrutiny; others grow stronger each dive season.

"Time Capsules, Not Tombs"
• Each submerged site locks away plant DNA, climate clues, and metallurgical experiments.
• Excavating with lasers and ROVs can harvest data without disturbing sacred spaces

Yet the larger truth stands tall even under 120 meters of water: humans have always been coastal innovators, charting the edge between harvest and hazard.

Will future historians dredge up our drowned skylines and wonder why we built so close to the tide? Perhaps—unless we learn now from Pavlopetri's narrow stone lanes, from Doggerland's vanished rivers, from sanctuaries that glittered along India's shores. The sea has already shown us the cost of forgetfulness. In its depths, it also holds the blueprint of resilience.

Take a breath, adjust your mask, and descend—the next discovery could be yours.

Part II: Evidence of Forgotten Genius

Chapter 4: Ancient Technologies That Shouldn't Exist

Why does the timeline of human ingenuity look like Swiss cheese, full of yawning holes that official history tries to ignore? Each time archaeologists pry open an ancient wreck, unseal a forgotten tomb, or run a laser scanner across a weather-blasted wall, another impossibility tumbles out. Welcome to the chapter in which we dig through three of the most unsettling finds on record—and invite you to decide whether they are lucky flukes or scattered fragments of a sophisticated era that simply slipped through the cracks.

The Antikythera Mechanism

How do you hide a mechanical computer in plain sight for two thousand years?

Every diver who visits the little island chain between Crete and southern Greece looks for sponge, but in the spring of 1900, one of them hauled up a lump of bronze so corroded that it seemed worthless scrap. Inside that barnacle-encrusted nodule lurked the oldest surviving geared device on Earth—a shoebox-sized contraption now called the **Antikythera Mechanism.**

What it did

- Star calendar: A front dial once mapped the daily journey of the sun, moon, and five visible planets through the zodiac.

- Eclipse oracle: A rotatable rear dial predicted lunar and solar eclipses decades in advance.

- Olympic timer: Yet another pointer kept track of Pan-Hellenic games on a four-year loop—a built-in sports calendar.

Even with more than half its parts missing, researchers have logged thirty-seven meshing bronze wheels. The largest boasts 223 triangular teeth cut so precisely that they still glide under light torque—a level of accuracy not duplicated again until Renaissance clock makers.

> ***The Sub-Millimeter Secret***
> *Modern X-ray tomography shows the gaps between opposing gear teeth average just 0.2 mm—narrow enough that a single sheet of paper would jam the mechanism. This tolerance rivals 18th-century marine chronometers, obliterating the myth that Hellenistic artisans relied on guesswork.*

Why it matters

- **Cognitive leap.** The machine converts linear time into rotating ratios—abstract mathematics hardened in bronze.

- **Invisible lineage.** Nobody starts with a masterpiece. The mechanism hints at an entire workshop tradition whose earlier models are lost.

- **Knowledge bottleneck.** When Rome absorbed Greece, skilled mechanics vanished from the record. The scientific revolution had to reinvent what once ticked away on a merchant ship.

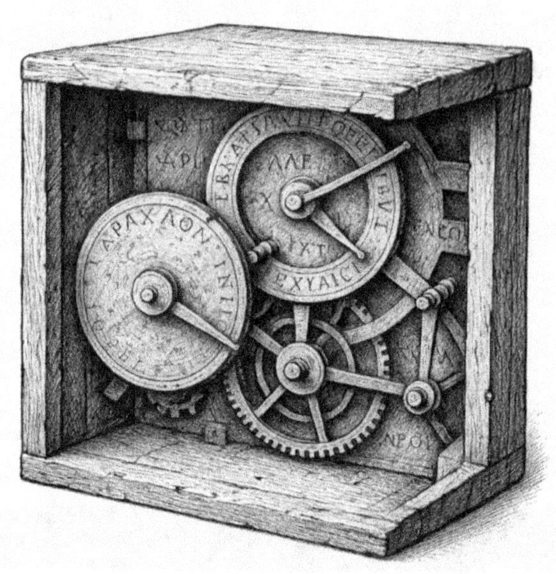

Faded Greek inscriptions on a cut wooden case

Ancient Surgical Tools & Metallurgy

If "primitive" surgeons could suture nerves and extract cataracts, what else have we underestimated?

Open the standard history text, and you'll read that antiseptic surgery began in the 19th century. Yet buried temple libraries and battlefield graves tell a sharper story—one forged in remarkably advanced metals.

Egypt's Bronze Scalpel & the Iron That Didn't Rust

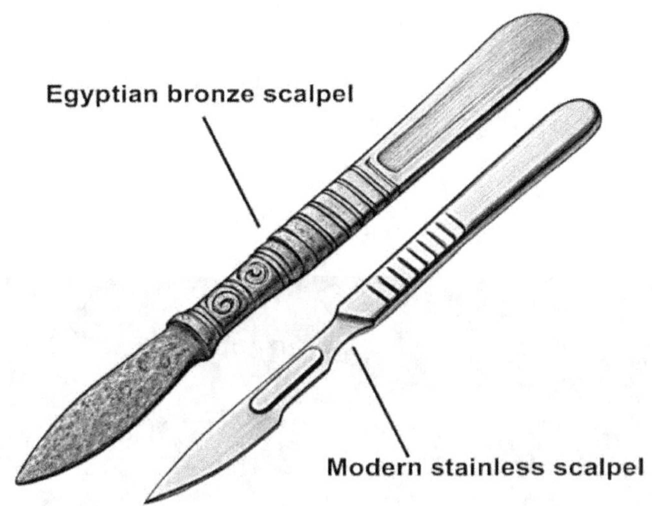

Old Kingdom reliefs show physicians brandishing knives identical in silhouette to modern bistouries. Metallographic tests on excavated examples reveal a tin-rich bronze alloy that holds an edge longer than many 19th-century carbon steels. Even stranger, a ceremonial surgical blade from Saqqara contains meteoritic nickel-iron—proof that smiths could cold-work extraterrestrial metal without forging furnaces hot enough to melt it.

Sushruta's Armamentarium

Across the Arabian Sea, Sanskrit texts list **125 named instruments** in use 2,600 years ago: fine-bore needles, spoon-shaped ear knives, and compound forceps for extracting broken arrowheads. The steel was crucible-born, quenched, and tempered in carbon-controlled furnaces—an early cousin of what later Europeans would brand "Damascus steel."

Roman Field Hospitals & Bronze Bone-Saws

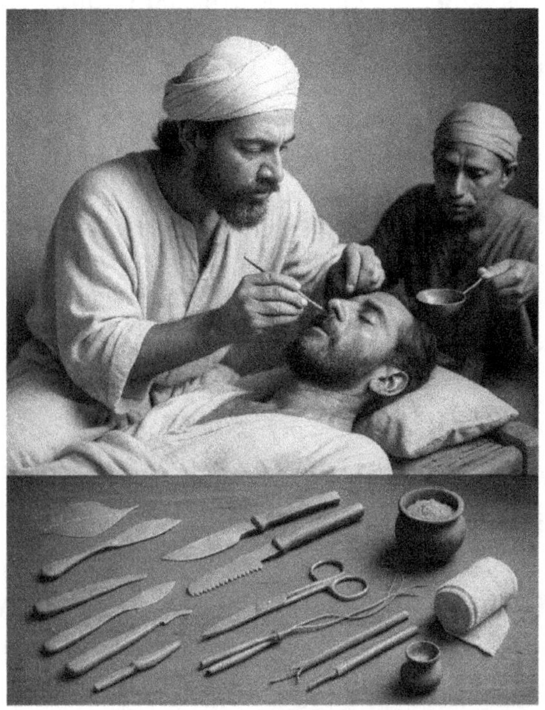

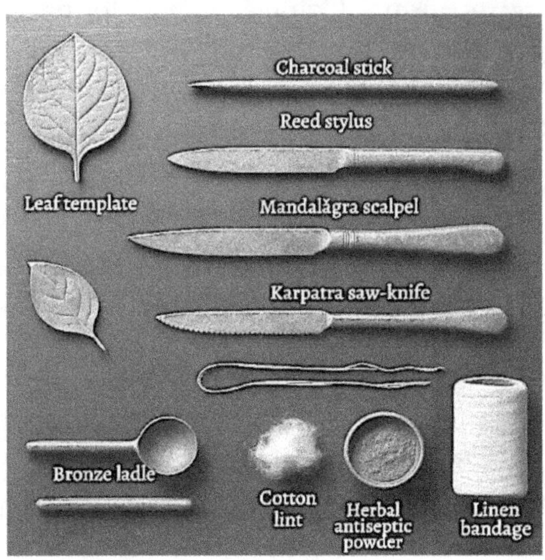

The best-preserved medical kit—unearthed at Pompeii—contains over 40 instruments: toothed three-jaw forceps for bullet extraction, catheters with interchangeable nozzles, and a serrated cupping globe used to draw blood to the surface (primitive vacuum therapy). Their survival owes everything to a metallurgical sweet spot—12 percent tin bronze—that resists infection-, breeding verdigris.

Metallurgy in Context

1. **Ore mastery.** Smelters balanced tin, arsenic, or carbon to tailor hardness—a hands-on grasp of phase diagrams millennia before academic metallurgy.

2. **Heat treatment.** Quenching, annealing, and work-hardening appear in workshop debris layers.

3. **Lost-wax precision.** Complex hollow forms for scalpels and forceps were cast via cire-perdue, matching today's investment casting tolerances.

The mystery of precision stonework

When a 100-ton block meets a Bronze-Age toolkit, something doesn't add up.

Few experiences recalibrate a visitor's sense of possibility like standing at the foot of a wall whose joints are so tight you cannot slide a credit card between blocks taller than a truck. Three sites illustrate the puzzle.

Sacsayhuamán (Peru)

Cyclopean ramparts weave together limestone polygons—some exceed 120 tons—without mortar. Measured gap: less than 0.05 mm on average. Engineers attempting laser scans struggle because the seams reflect as a single surface.

The Trilithon (Baalbek, Lebanon)

Three foundation stones weighing 800 – 1,000 tons each rest on sub-blocks that themselves top 300 tons. No Bronze Age hoist, sled, or ramp theory convincingly explains how they cleared a four-meter terrace wall and seated flush.

"Rosetta-Stone" Drill Marks in Egypt

Inside the Serapeum of Saqqara, granite sarcophagi exhibit tubular drill holes whose feed rates—judged by spiral groove depth—imply pressures impossible to achieve with copper bits twirled by hand.

How Could It Be Done?

1. **Abrasive cable saws.** Sand-slinging bronze wires can slice limestone, but bog down in quartz-rich granite.

2. **Thermal shock.** Repeated fire-quench cycles fracture surfaces yet leave no sign of the razor-straight joins observed.

> **Fifty-Micron Fit**
> At contact points, opposing stones mirror one another with deviations smaller than a human hair. Weathering has not widened those seams after half a millennium of earthquakes.

3. **Sonic or chemical softening?** No residue supports these fringe ideas, but the precision gap keeps them alive in debate.

Whatever the method, three attributes reappear world-wide:

- **Pre-assembly modeling.** Blocks were pre-shaped off-site—likely via full-scale templates—then locked into place with almost zero on-site correction.

- **Earthquake resilience.** Offset joints dissipate seismic waves better than modern rigid concrete.

- **Tool marks vanish.** Final polishing erased manufacturing fingerprints, as if ancient engineers wanted the mystery to remain.

The Antikythera Mechanism proves the ancients could encode celestial laws in bronze calculus. Surgical kits from Egypt to India reveal an anatomical literacy that would not reappear in the West for two millennia. Megalithic walls set with hair-line joins challenge our heavy-machinery chauvinism. Each domain—clockwork, metallurgy, stone craft—displays a common signature: **mathematics translated into matter with an elegance that makes our age uneasy.**

So we stand at a crossroads, reader in hand. Do we patch these anomalies into the margins of the existing script, or admit the script itself might be missing entire chapters? In the pages ahead, we will weigh more evidence for a civilization that mastered science, medicine, and engineering, only to scatter its knowledge like sparks in the wind. Keep your eyes on those sparks; they still burn.

Chapter 5

Maps of the Impossible

If a single sheet of vellum drawn in 1513 can reveal coastlines no human eye should yet have seen, what else might be hiding in the archives of history-that-never-was?

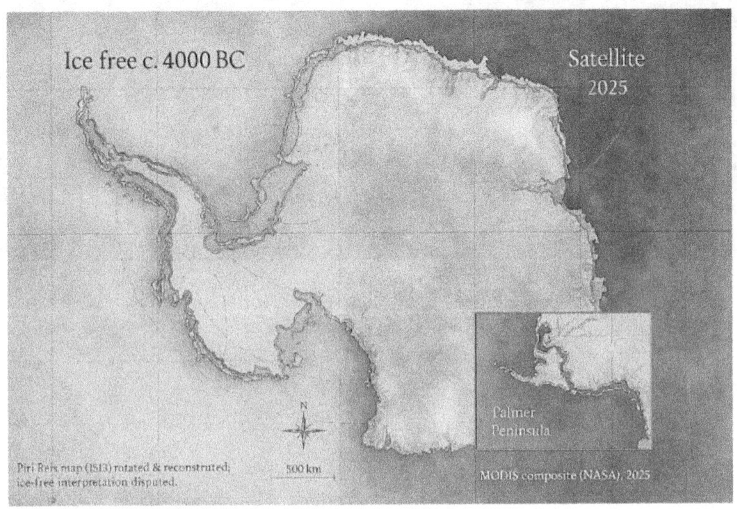

A Gazelle-Skin Enigma

In 1929, museum workers in Istanbul unrolled a fragmentary world map painted on gazelle hide. Along its jagged lower edge, unmistakable mountains, rivers, and inlets traced the true profile of Antarctica's Queen Maud Land—yet the southern continent would not be "discovered" for another three centuries.

An internal note scrawled in Ottoman Turkish revealed that the admiral Piri Reis had copied this coastline, and much else, from "ancient charts." Modern seismic surveys completed in 1949 proved that the mountains matched the land *beneath* today's mile-thick ice, implying the source charts were drawn when that coast was still ice-free, sometime before 4000 BC.

The Piri Reis Puzzle
- *Antarctic shores plotted 300 years before their "discovery"*
- *Sub-glacial topography matches 20th-century seismic data*
- *Only possible during the last Ice-Age meltdown (13 000–4000 BC)*
- *Admiral admits he merely compiled "old charts"*

The Piri Reis Map and Ice Age coastlines

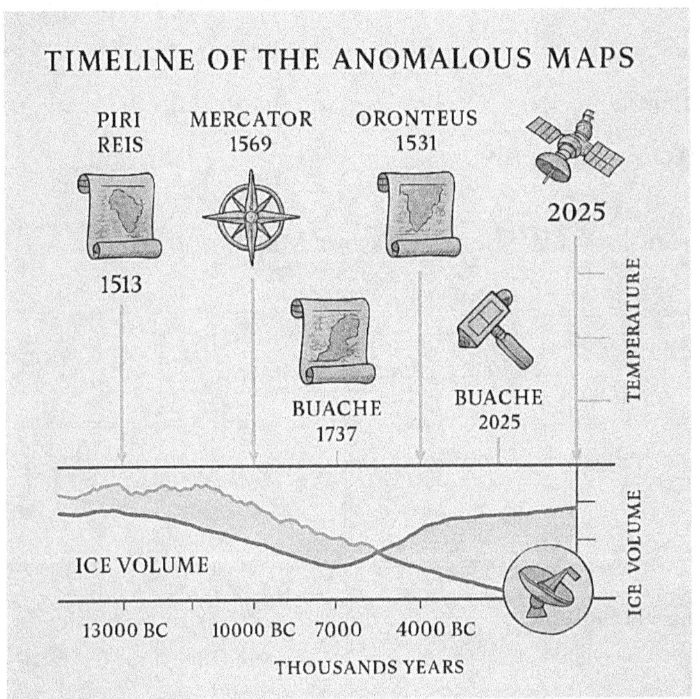

Reis was not alone. The Oronteus Finaeus world map of 1531 shows Antarctica ringed with estuaries and navigable rivers. Gerard Mercator's 1569 atlas repeats the feat, adding capes and islands still recognized today. And Philippe Buache's chart of 1737 divides the continent into eastern and western landmasses, separated by an ice-free seaway later confirmed by satellite altimetry.

Ice-core and ocean-floor data indicate that Antarctica's coast oscillated between temperate and glacial states during the terminal Ice Age; the Buache source seems to date from the warmest pulse

(~13,000 BC), Oronteus from an intermediate stage, and Reis from the last gasp of open water around 6000 years ago. The implication is a *continuous* surveying enterprise spanning millennia—a project far beyond any culture recognized by conventional history.

Chronology Of The Anomalous Maps

Map	Underlying survey epoch	Climatic state	Key revelations
Buache (1737)	c. 13,000 BC	Ice-free	Central seaway, full river systems
Oronteus Finaeus (1531)	c. 10,000 BC	Coastal ice absent, interior cap	Mountains & estuaries
Mercator (1569)	c. 6000 BC	Expanding ice	Capes & islands now buried
Piri Reis (1513)	c. 4000 BC	Coastline freezing over	Queen Maud Land profile

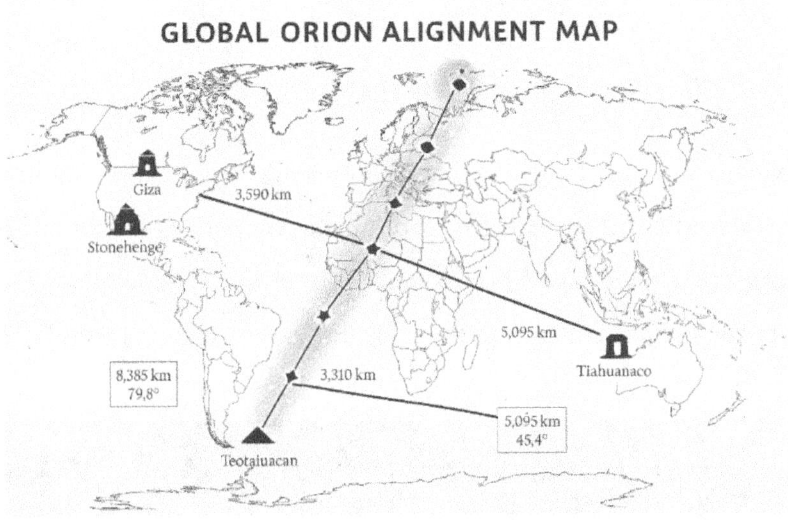

Accurate world maps hint at planet-wide exploration, but ground-level clues point to something deeper: **a deliberate geometry linking sacred sites across continents.**

- **The Orion Blueprint.** Join Giza, Stonehenge, Teotihuacan, and Tiahuanaco on a Mercator projection, add a central point in the mid-Atlantic, and the network sketches the constellation of Orion's Belt.

- **Druids, Ceques, and Geodesy.** Celtic centers in Britain were laid out with surprising geodetic precision, echoing the ceque lines that radiate from Cusco's Temple of the Sun. Both systems treat the landscape as a mandala where rulership depends on *measuring the Earth.*

- **The Earth-Crystal Hypothesis.** Soviet researchers Goncharov, Morozov, and Makarov mapped nodes of seismic and magnetic activity onto a dual dodecahedron–icosahedron grid whose "position one" sits beneath the Great Pyramid.

Meanwhile, on Peru's Nazca pampa, mile-long arrows, radiating trapezoids, and animal effigies double as sight-lines to Orion's Belt and other asterisms. The workmanship required aerial planning—yet the earliest confirmed flight over Nazca occurred in the 1920s.

> *Cusco ceques → quarter the Inca realm*
> *Nazca spider → tracks Orion for 1500 years*
> *Atlantic "Orion" → distances encode Earth's circumference*

Ancient Cartography vs. Modern Satellites

Hand-drawn Renaissance charts anticipated discoveries that would wait for 20th-century radar and space imagery:

Feature	First mapped by the "ancients"	Scientific confirmation
Sub-glacial mountain ranges in Queen Maud Land	Piri Reis fragment 1513	Seismic echo-sounding 19 49
Ross Sea river deltas	Oronteus Finaeus 1 531	Core drilling: temperate sediments
Falkland Islands latitude	Piri Reis	Captain John Da vis, 1592
Mid-Atlantic Ridge island (submerged)	Piri Reis	Bathymetry & satellite altimetry

Today, software can overlay Buache's ice-free seaway atop radar-derived bedrock, revealing a near-perfect match. In effect, the old maps function like "black-box recordings" preserved through the Dark Ages, only now fully legible with orbital sensors.

Who Were the Surveyors?

Mainstream models claim civilization "began" around 4000 BC, yet the **maps of the impossible** say otherwise. To chart an ice-free Antarctica required:

- Ocean-going fleets or airborne platforms,
- Spherical trigonometry for longitude,
- Coordinated observations have been maintained over thousands of years.

These are the hallmarks of a **literate, scientific culture**—one erased by the climatic whiplash that ended the Ice Age. Mythic memory preserves them as the Viracochas of the Andes, the Apkallu of Mesopotamia, the *Magicians of the Gods* who emerge after a cataclysm to reboot the world.

Their fingerprints suggest an audacious project: mapping the planet, then encoding that knowledge in monuments, geoglyphs, and story so that future generations—*us*—could one day recover the library. The cartographers of the deep past may be gone, but their charts still whisper directions for those who care to listen.

If a single vellum fragment can overturn an entire chronology, what riches await on the next dusty shelf? Perhaps the greatest secret is not that the ancients knew the world, but that they believed we, too, would one day be ready to rediscover it.

Chapter 6

Messages from the Ancients

What if every cryptic parchment, every stone that sings to the horizon, and every tale of a world-engulfing flood is part of the same encrypted letter—one addressed to us? What might the senders have been desperate for us to remember? And why does that message still throb, half-buried, beneath the static of modern noise?

The Voynich Manuscript: A Book No One Can Read

Pull a single volume from a medieval library and you expect brittle Latin or rounded Greek. Yet the Voynich Manuscript greets you with coils of elegant, utterly alien script, spiralling plants that never sprouted in any botanist's field guide, and star maps whose logic eludes the most seasoned astronomer. Carbon dating pins its vellum to the early fifteenth century – roughly **1404–1438 CE** – but the text refuses to confess its secret. Cryptographers from Queen Elizabeth I's code-breakers to twenty-first-century super-computers have deployed their arsenals on the pages, only to retreat in silence.

Every few years, a fresh contender steps into the ring: perhaps it is an ingenious cipher designed to conceal heretical medical lore; perhaps a shorthand proto-Romance language; perhaps an artful hoax whispered into being by a Renaissance trickster. A 2024 linguistic reassessment, for instance, claimed the underlying tongue resembles a **calligraphic**

proto-Romance with dozens of scribal abbreviations. The ink dries, scholars debate, and the story resets. The code still breathes.

But the manuscript's stubborn opacity is itself a clue. Here is a culture convinced that knowledge could—and should—be preserved for those with the correct key. Imagine a Europe reeling from plague, schism, and war: if you believed ancient wisdom was under threat, wouldn't you lock it inside a cipher strong enough to outlive every catastrophe?

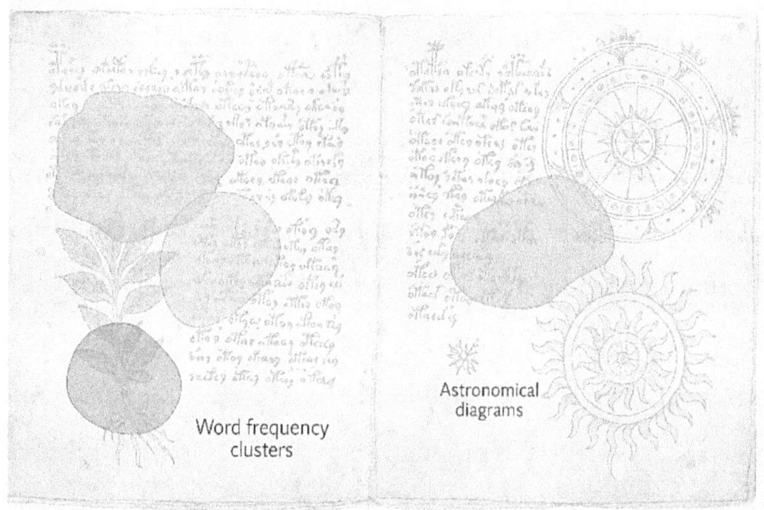

In short, the Voynich Manuscript is not a riddle to amuse code-breakers. It is a survival capsule. The ancients did not want us to read it easily; they wanted us to care enough to try for centuries.

Megalithic Alignments and Star Maps

Walk the circumference of Stonehenge at dawn, stand exactly at the monument's heart, and watch the midsummer sun rise itself above the Heel Stone. The first shaft of light slices clean through the sarsen corridor, as it has for five millennia. The architecture is an almanac in limestone.

Now follow the ley of light across oceans and epochs. In Brittany, mile-long stone rows at Carnac point to lunar standstills; in Malta, Mnajdra's trilithon frames equinoctial sunrise; in Peru, the Intihuatana of Machu Picchu tethers the December solstice noon; in Sudan's desert, the calendar circle of Nabta Playa predates the Egyptian pyramids by a thousand years. Polaris moves, dynasties fall, but the monuments refuse to forget.

At Göbekli Tepe—a hilltop sanctuary raised twelve thousand years ago—the animal reliefs on Pillar 43 form a sky chart. When the carvings are superimposed on the heavens, the vulture, scorpion, and bending ibis line up with the constellations of Sagittarius, Scorpius, and Libra close to the north celestial pole as it appeared in **10,950 BCE,** near the very date of the Younger Dryas climatic whip-crack. The artisans not only tracked the stars; they time-stamped their warning in stone.

The Geometry of Intention

Megalithic sites are not haphazardly oriented; they are obsessively, even mathematically, precise. Surveyors mapping megaliths in northwest Europe discovered that the azimuths of key sight-lines fall into discrete bundles: solar, lunar, and axial-precessional. The implication is staggering: across thousands of kilometres, cultures shared a unified geodesic and astronomical vocabulary. Either a single civilisation once spanned that territory, or knowledge travellers—priest-engineers?—carried the canon from site to site like sparks leaping a firebreak.

> ### *The Global Megalith Code*
>
> - *Cardinal orientation: ±0.3° average error in pyramid faces, passage-graves, and henges.*
> - *Solstitial corridors: aligned to sunrise/sunset at ±3 days of annual extremes.*
> - *Lunar nodes: major/minor standstill lines appear in approximately one-third of surveyed monuments.*
> - *Precessional fingerprints: baseline angles (for example 23.5°) encode axial tilt epochs*

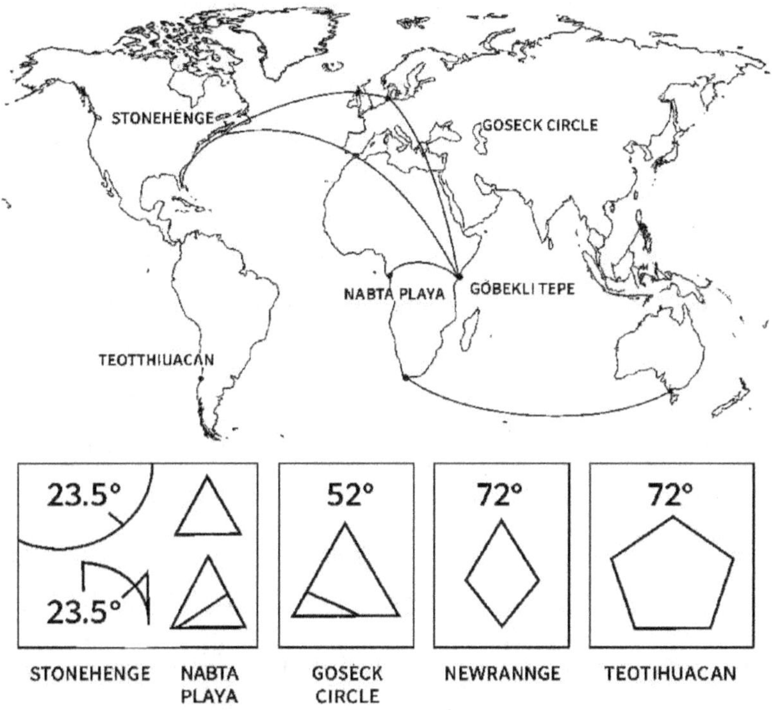

Neolithic Network — The Angles of Ancient Time

Consider the possibility that these structures are waypoints in a planetary observatory network designed to outlast its builders. Even if you lost the manual, you could reconstruct the system by watching where the stones point. The ancients solved the ultimate technological dilemma: how to transmit data when storage media rot and languages die. They built their hard drives out of mountains.

Myths as Memory: Decoding Flood Legends

If stone is the ancients' hardware, myth is their software. In every hemisphere, we hear the same refrain: waters rose, mountains vanished, and a remnant survived by foreknowledge and craft. The Sumerian *Ziusudra*, the Hebrew *Noah*, the Indian *Manu*, the Greek *Deucalion*, the Mayan *Iguana-Woman*, the Aboriginal *Tiddalik*—stories separated by oceans converge on one super-event.

Geology bears them out. Around **12,800 years ago,** Earth lurched into the Younger Dryas, a near-glacial cold snap possibly triggered by cometary fragments that raked North America, scattering nano-diamonds and melt-glass across two continents. Then, abruptly, the ice reversed course. Between 11,300 and 11,000 years ago, Meltwater Pulse 1B added up to eleven metres of sea-level in as little as two and a half centuries. Coastal plains—prime real estate for early civilisations—were drowned. Recent modelling suggests total post-glacial rise reached **38 metres ($\approx$ 125 ft)** before stabilising.

Why do temples and story cycles obsess over celestial alignments just when oceans were consuming the shoreline? Because the sky and sea were joined in the same catastrophe. A cosmic impact darkened the heavens; ice sheets cracked; deluge followed. Cultures that mastered astronomy could predict both the impact season and the flood's tempo. Their wisdom became religion, their observatories became shrines, and their warnings became myth.

CATACLYSMS & COASTLINES:
A Hypothetical Younger Dryas Comet Scenario

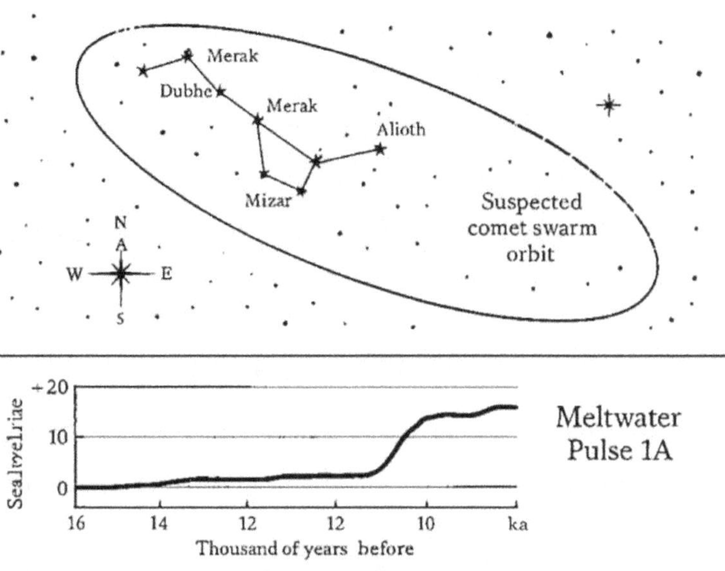

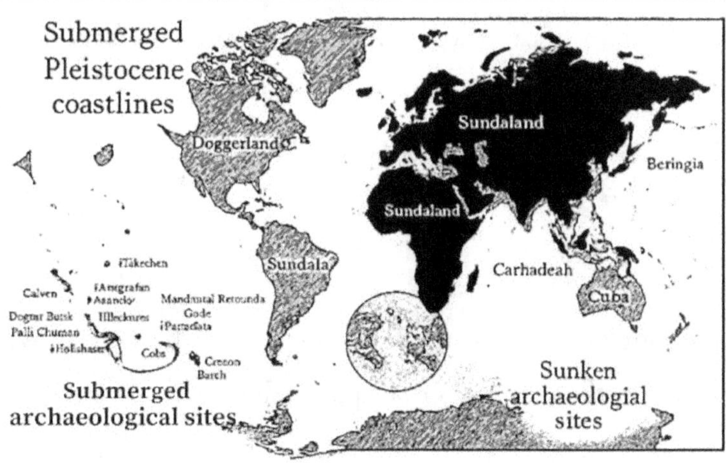

We Are Part of This Investigation

The ancients did not design their messages for passive consumption; they engineered them to provoke questing minds. The Voynich Manuscript withholds its alphabet so that each generation, sharpening its decipherment tools, discovers something about linguistics and cognition. The megaliths lock data in baseline alignments so that only sky-watchers—citizens, not priests—can relearn the great rhythms. Flood myths frighten and fascinate, so we will model climates and measure seas.

Look again at the pattern. When the planet reels, sky-literate societies endure. They store knowledge redundantly—ink for short memory, stone for the longue durée, story for the soul. That trifold strategy is a blueprint we can still adopt.

In the chapters ahead, we will weigh more artefacts of genius: antediluvian spheres whose grooves mimic wheels, desert geoglyphs visible only from the stratosphere, algorithms encoded in mythic genealogies. But before we march on, linger a moment in the hush of these three transmissions:

1. **A book no one can read**—proof that the written word can outlive the languages that spawned it.

2. **Monoliths that summon the sun**—proof that architecture can outlast the cultures that formed the blueprint.

3. **Stories that survive the sea**—proof that the imagination can outlast every library on Earth.

Together they whisper a single imperative:

"Observe the heavens, remember the waters, and pass the torch intact."

Will we listen?

Part III: The Hidden Orders

Chapter 7

Secret Societies and Lost Knowledge

Why do certain emblems echo across centuries?
Who keeps the blueprints of worlds that vanished beneath flood, fire, and creed?
Are today's whispered cabals mere phantoms—or custodians of archives older than memory itself?

Welcome to a guided descent through stone corridors and sealed libraries, where the trail of suppressed wisdom passes from crusading knights to modern fraternities, brushes the Vatican's miles of vaults, and resurfaces in the conspiracy folklore of the Illuminati and Skull & Bones. Keep your wits sharpened: what follows is equal parts documented fact and contested legend, and the border between the two is the very ground these societies have learned to patrol.

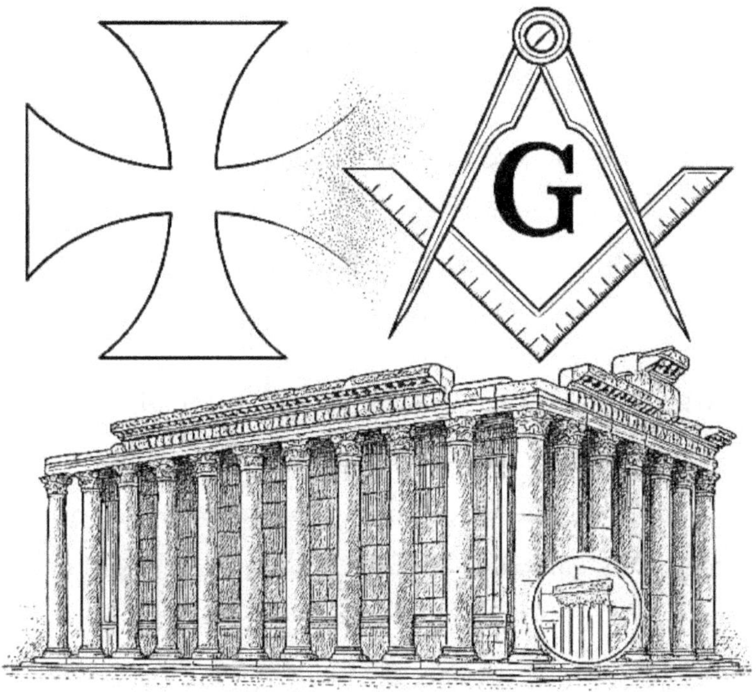

SYMBOLIC CONTINUUM
—Templar Cross to Freemason Square & Compass over Baalbek (Bacchus Temple)

Formed in the early twelfth century, the Poor Fellow-Soldiers of Christ and the Temple of Solomon pledged themselves to protect pilgrims in the Holy Land. Yet within two generations, they had evolved into Europe's first multinational corporation, complete with a diplomatic courier network, fortified commanderies, and the most sophisticated ledger-based banking system of the age.

Hidden repositories. When the Order was finally suppressed in 1307, royal agents seized vast armories of gold and parchment. Most of the financial ledgers were burned—yet tantalizing references remain to "arkoe" of scrolls spirited from Jerusalem, rumored to contain architectural schemes and star-codes traced back to a lost antediluvian priesthood. Modern Freemasons point to an unbroken lineage: Templar Grand Masters are depicted in the reliefs of Baalbek's Temple of Bacchus, where hand-signals perfectly match the *Entered Apprentice* and *Fellowcraft* grades of the craft today.

Trans-Atlantic clues. Crosses identical to the Templar device appear on Olmec basalt heads and Mayan façades. Whether this is evidence of direct contact or a far older, global symbol-bank, the Templars merely inherited remains contested—but the multiplicity of appearances hints at travelers who carried sacred geometry rather than swords.

Templar Signatures to Watch For
- *Red, paw-shaped cross (croix pattée).*
- *Equal-armed Saint-Andrew cross (found shockingly on the Pre-Columbian Pyramid of the Magician at Uxmal).*
- *Twin columns guarding a portal, later absorbed by Masonic tracing boards.*

The treasure that mattered. Legends fixate on wagons of bullion escaping France, yet contemporary depositions obsess over a different loss: *books.* Interrogators demanded to know what texts Jacques de Molay had removed from Paris. No answer satisfied them— perhaps because the answer lay far from Europe, in desert rock-cuts and mountain-caves already ancient in Templar eyes.

Freemasons – Operating Lodge or Operating System?

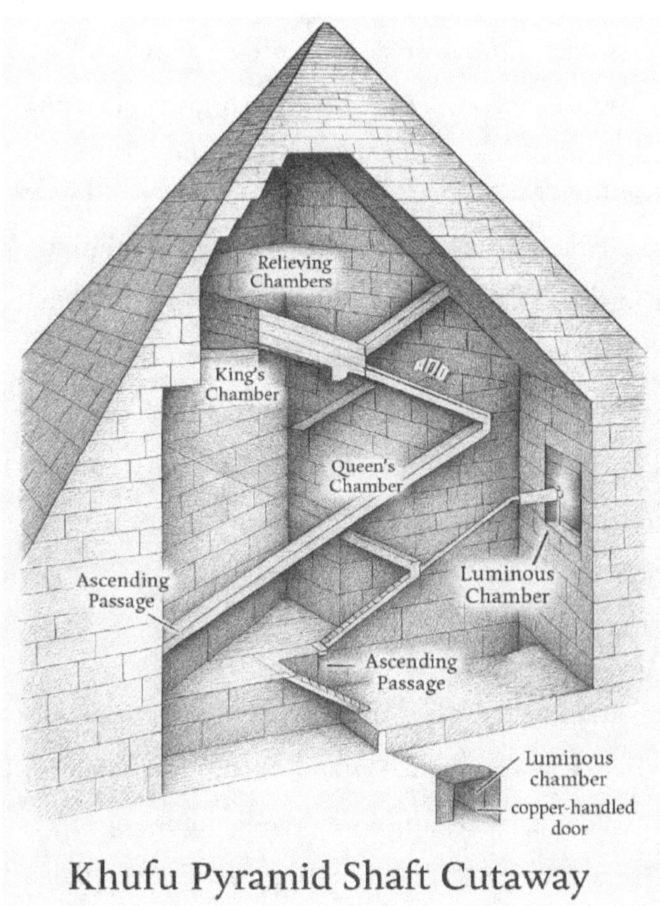

Khufu Pyramid Shaft Cutaway

When the medieval stonemason guilds blossomed into speculative philosophy, they did so draped in Templar mythos and Solomon's cryptic floor plans. The fraternity's core ritual is an allegorical *search for the Lost Word*—a key the Knights allegedly carried out of Jerusalem.

Baalbek's Masonic classroom. Inside the Temple of Bacchus, seventeenth-century travelers noted the *Seal of Solomon* etched into architraves and a carved figure silently gesturing the Apprentice grip. Modern Masonic historians read the entire site as a stone textbook: a primer on how stellar time-cycles and megalithic engineering interlock.

Giza's speaking shafts. In 1872, English engineer and lodge member Waynman Dixon "suspected" unseen tunnels behind the Queen's Chamber in the Great Pyramid. He chiselled until his tool punched through into a nine-inch conduit that rose into darkness—the same shaft that robotics pioneer Rudolf Gantenbrink would re-explore 121 years later, discovering a miniature limestone door with copper handles and an unexplained gap beneath. Masons cite the episode as a literal enactment of the quest motif: a concealed portal guarding lost master-plans.

Enoch the architect. Tucked inside old lodge lectures is a tale of the patriarch Enoch engraving a "Grand Secret" on a white stone and hiding it below ground to resist the coming Deluge. Victorian Cyclopedias reinforce the link, asserting that Enoch "taught men the art of building" before surrendering his Grand Master's office to

Lamech. Compare that with Egyptian papyri that speak of a chest of flint in Heliopolis preserving "the number of the secret chambers of Thoth" for Pharaoh Khufu to copy—clearly, multiple cultures remember archivists preparing blueprints for a future age.

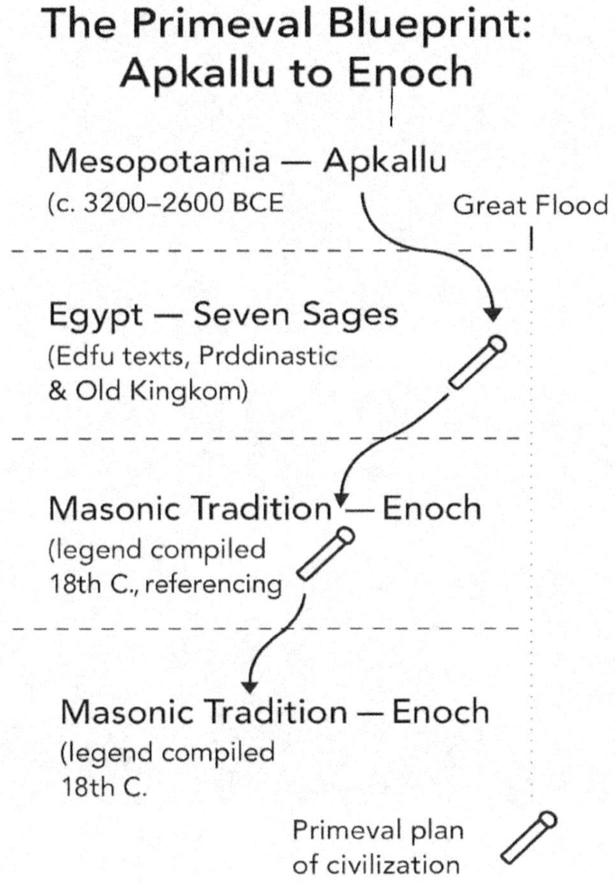

Technology or theology? Arab chronicler Ibn Abd El Hakem maintained that inside Giza lay "arms which did not rust" and "glass which might be bent but not broken," guarded by statues that could stun intruders with sound and light. Whether we interpret this literally as lost engineering or symbolically as metaphysical force, the message is the same: deep knowledge demands deep protection.

The Vatican's Forbidden Vaults

Pax in Tenebris — The Vatican Vault

Beneath Rome, 85 kilometres of shelving store manuscripts sealed until the pontiff decrees otherwise. Papal bulls, inquisitorial dossiers, and entire archives of defunct orders (including Templar property trials) lie off-limits to independent scholars.

Layers of secrecy. The Archivum Secretum was formalised by Pope Paul V in 1612, yet its roots reach back to Constantine's *scrinium*—a chest said to hold apostolic letters. Among treasures catalogued but unseen are:

1. **A dossier on the trial of Galileo.**

2. **The parchment of Chinon**, absolving Templar leaders in 1308.

3. Registers of heretical texts confiscated after the Council of Nicaea.

Researchers allowed inside can request just **three folders per day**; photography is prohibited. Such bottlenecks foster suspicion that uncomfortable pre-Christian narratives—Atlantean cosmogonies, perhaps—are being rationed or redacted rather than merely conserved.

Convergence at the crossroads. Note the uncanny symmetry: Masonic lore points to "the Vault beneath the Temple"; Templar tradition hints at scrolls exiled to safe western repositories; Egyptian priests speak of a Hall of Records under the paws of the Sphinx where the gods' plans were copied for later ages. The *geography* differs, but the *concept* is identical: hide civilisation's instruction-manual until humanity regains the moral maturity to wield it.

Field Guide to Restricted Repositories

Repository	Official Purpose	Rumoured Contents	Access Gatekeepers
Vatican Secret Archive	Church diplomacy & doctrine	Pre-Nicene gospels; Templar ledgers	Papal Prefect
Sphinx Hall of Records	Ritual crypt	Maps of Atlantis; star-charts from 10,500 BC	Ministry of Antiquities
Masonic Royal Arch Vault	Allegory of resurrection	Enochian pillar; "Lost Word" cipher	Chapter High-Priest

Every vault professes piety; every padlock whispers panic.

Modern Myths – Illuminati & Skull & Bones

Illuminati: From Enlightenment Lodge to Pop-Culture Villain

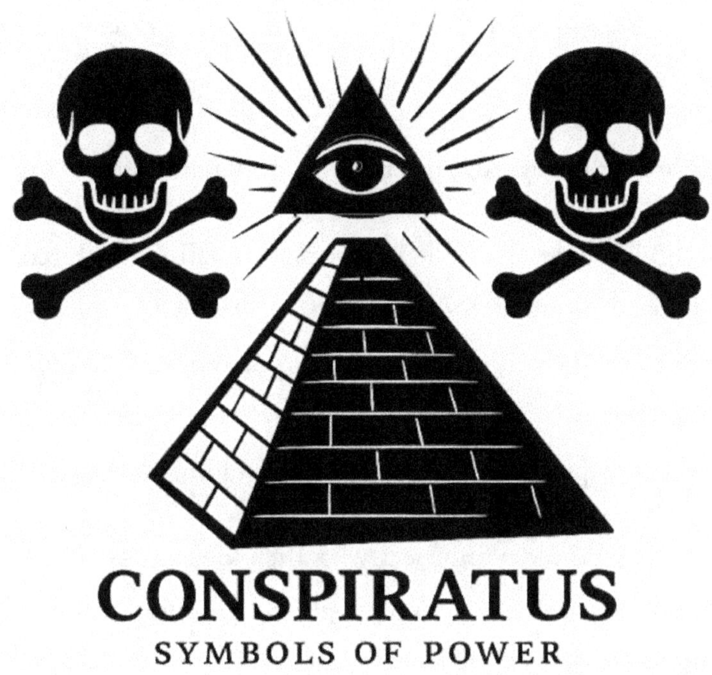

Adam Weishaupt's Enlightenment cell (founded 1776) sought to replace superstition with reason, infiltrating Masonic lodges to accelerate reform. Bavaria banned the order within a decade, but its ghost walked on—fertilised by nineteenth-century pamphleteers and twentieth-century pulp thrillers until "Illuminati" became shorthand for any unseen board of puppet-masters. Unlike the lineage-rich Templars or Masons, its paper-trail is thin; its notoriety, thick.

The resonance. Conspiracy literature eagerly projects Illuminati influence backwards onto the Templars and forward onto bankers, shipping tycoons, and even NASA. Whether or not the heredity is factual, the archetype fulfills a cultural need: a single cabal to weave disparate anomalies—rust-free swords, bent glass, robot-guarded tombs—into one overarching plotline.

Skull & Bones: An American Echo Chamber

Founded in 1832 at Yale, this collegiate society ritualises death (coffin initiations), empire (Bonesmen dominated the OSS, CIA, and several White Houses), and—critically—**information control**. Members swear to place fraternity loyalty above church or nation, a direct inversion of the Templar vow to defend Christendom.

Where does their mythology intersect with the older orders? Both the Bones tomb and Masonic Halls deploy **silent symbols**—hourglasses, crossed bones, owls—to programme initiates into time-based thinking. Both cultivate *archival privileges*: Bones curators maintain dossiers on every member, stored in locked towers; Masonic Grand Lodges secure minute-books inaccessible to profane eyes.

Curators of Cataclysmic Memory

Why do these societies cling to fragments of impossibly old history? A clue emerges in Egyptian *Edfu Building Texts,* which describe survivors of a flood carrying "the words of the Sages" to new temple sites. Parallel Mesopotamian tablets credit the *Apkallu* with rebuilding civilisation after the deluge, while Arab chroniclers insist the pyramids hide indestructible manuals on "astrology, arithmetic, geometry and medicine … everything that is and shall be from the beginning to the end of time".

Secret societies, then, can be read as **memory guilds**—vaulting endangered data across dark ages until astronomy, ethics, and engineering are safe for release. The Templars may have uncovered plans beneath Solomon's stables; eighteenth-century Freemasons chiselled allegory over those blueprints; Vatican archivists locked dissenting gospels in climate-controlled drawers; Skull & Bones distilled fixation on apocalypse into policy seminars.

Yet bottling knowledge invites stagnation—and the occasional explosion. Witness modern *forbidden archaeology*: artifacts placing *Homo sapiens* far deeper in time than textbooks allow are ignored or derided, their discoverers black-listed just as rigorously as any medieval heretic. The instinct to suppress paradigm-shifting data didn't die with Inquisitors; it migrated into peer-review committees.

The Archive Is Alive

Secret societies thrive because official history is a palimpsest: a rewritten scroll where every dynasty scrapes away prior ink. Someone must conserve erased lines, even if they sit in catacombs labelled "Do Not Enter." Templars, Freemasons, curial librarians, or collegiate fraternities—whatever their motives—serve as imperfect stewards of humanity's misplaced instruction-manual.

Our task is neither to worship nor to demonise them, but to recognise the pattern they illustrate:

1. Catastrophe resets civilisation.

2. Survivors cache knowledge in guarded vaults.

3. Custodians develop codes, rituals, and hierarchies to protect the caches.

4. Public curiosity eventually pries open a shaft, a drawer, or a database.

5. The paradigm shifts; a new cycle of concealment begins.

The next vault might yield an alloy that refuses rust, or a cosmos-graph that bends glass without breaking. When the seal finally slides, let us hope the hands that receive the treasure are steadier—and the vision broader—than before.

You have now traversed the coded chronicles of crusading knights, operative masons, cloistered archivists, and skull-bearing fraternities. The question lingers: Will you knock on their doors—or build a vault of your own?

Chapter 8

Forbidden Science

Why do the most tantalising breakthroughs arrive with the soft thud of a file drawer snapping shut?

Who decides which blueprints, bones, and brittle parchments see daylight—and which are locked away?

Welcome, investigator. From this point forward, you are not a passive reader; you are part of the inquiry. Together we will unspool three intertwined threads—breakthrough invention, buried artefact, and institutional gate-keeping—that weave a grand pattern of omission. By chapter's end, you will hold a sharper lens for spotting *why* entire chapters of humankind's story, and whole pages of technological genius, vanish in plain sight.

Nikola Tesla's "Lost" Inventions

When Nikola Tesla died in room 3327 of the New Yorker Hotel on 7 January 1943, federal agents arrived before the undertaker. They swept his trunks into a warehouse under the Alien Property Custodian. Many were later released to relatives, but two steamer trunks and at least one set of laboratory notebooks were **never** returned. Inside those missing containers lay the seed-corn of projects so audacious that even now they read like science fiction.

Blueprints Gone Walkabout

- **Wireless terrestrial power** Tesla's Wardenclyffe Tower was not merely a radio mast; its 57-ton copper topload and buried ground plate formed a resonant transformer able (in theory) to pump megawatt pulses through the planet's conductive strata. Eyewitnesses saw lamps glow miles from his Colorado lab with no wires attached.

- **Directed-energy "teleforce" device,** Tesla described a charged particle projector that could "melt airplane engines at 250 miles." He offered the idea to the U.S., U.K., and Yugoslavia; all declined officially. When the Cold War dawned, fragments of the concept resurfaced inside classified beam-weapons studies.

- **Mechanical resonance amplifier.** Journalists dubbed it the "earthquake machine" after Tesla bolted a hand-sized oscillator to a New York tenement beam and purportedly rattled the block. The tuning secrets vanished with his notes.

> ***Tesla's Missing Wardenclyffe Papers***
> - *Last logged in New York customs manifest, 1942*
> - *Described as "packet of 45 loose drawings, A2 size"*
> - *Contents indexed: coil geometries, earth current propagation tests, cost ledger*
> - *Chain of custody after 1943: unknown*

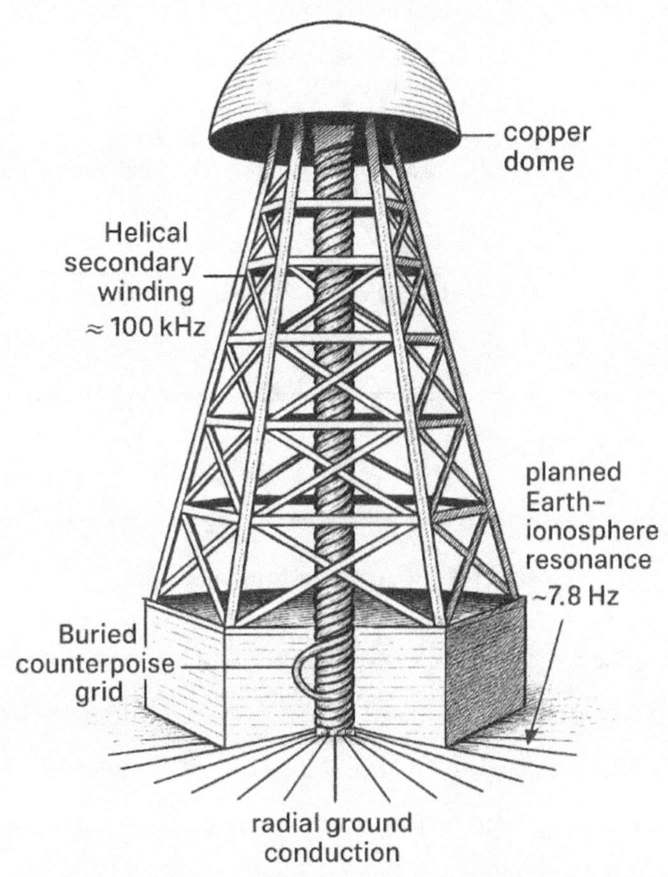

**Wardenclyffe Tower Resonant Transmission
Cutaway (Tesla, 1901)**

How a Visionary Becomes an Anomaly

Tesla's radical concepts threatened two entrenched empires: monopoly utilities (whose profits hinged on meters, not free energy) and military planners (who coveted, then classified, any device that could tilt future wars). The easiest way to neutralise both risks? Rebrand the inventor as an eccentric and quarantine his paperwork.

Key Tactics of Technical Burial

Tactic	Mechanism	Result
Over-classification	Label as "national security"	Public literature gap
Patent limbo	File but never prosecute patents	Idea fenced off yet unused
Character framing	"Mad scientist" press memes	Investor retreat

Suppressed Archaeological Finds

Archaeology sells itself as a canvas painted stroke by empirical stroke—yet whole swaths are scrubbed when they clash with the palette approved by gatekeepers. An undercurrent of "knowledge filtration" (the term coined by field insiders) sifts discoveries through the mesh of preconceived chronology.

The Table Mountain Relics

During California's 19th-century gold rush, miners drove drifts hundreds of metres into basalt-sealed gravels. From layers dated 33–55 million years, they hauled obsidian spearpoints, mortars, pestles, and a human femur. State geologist J. D. Whitney published a monograph; a Smithsonian authority countered that the finds "could not exist" and *therefore* must be mistakes. Display cases were pulled, specimens boxed, funding dried up, and the episode evaporated from textbooks.

Checklist: How Evidence Gets "Disappeared"

1. Question the finder's credentials, not the strata.

2. Deny museum access to independent examiners.

3. Starve dissenters of excavation permits or radiometric budgets.

4. Declare the matter "settled" in a single review paper—then mis-shelve the original report.

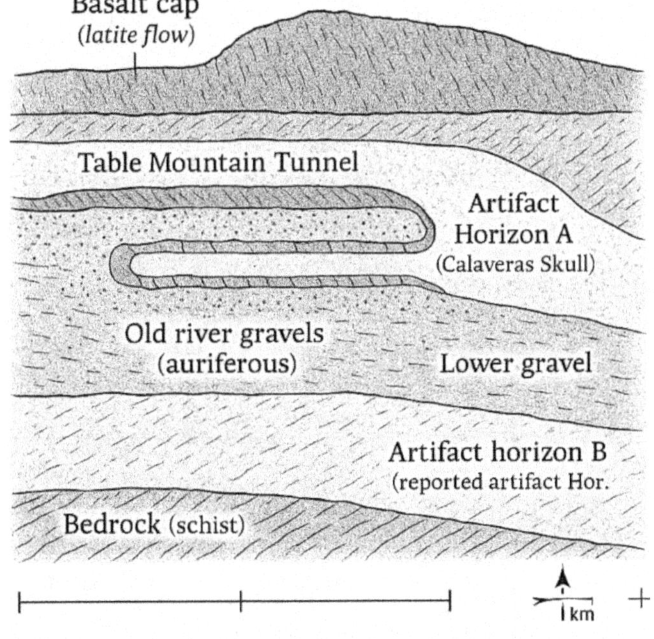

Table Mountain Tunnel Cross-Section with Reported Artifact Horizons

Hueyatlaco, Mexico—250,000 BP or Career Suicide?

Geochronologist Virginia Steen-McIntyre dated sophisticated blades near Puebla to a quarter-million years, ten times the accepted age for anatomically modern toolmakers. Publication was delayed, grants evaporated, and her academic post dissolved. The site remains in limbo, a case study in professional penalty for chronological disobedience.

The Pyramid That Shouldn't Exist

In Bosnia's Visoko Valley rises a terraced hill whose gradient, orientation, and quartz-rich concrete blocks suggest purposeful design. Early core samples returned Pleistocene age markers; excavators requested wider digs. International critics, having never set foot at the pit face, lobbied journals to brand the project a hoax and urged professional bodies to blacklist participants. The hill endures—either the largest man-made pyramid on Earth or an inconvenient orphan awaiting admission to the archaeological family tree.

Timeline of Anomalous Finds

Date (CE)	Location	Anomaly	Suppression Trigger
1840 s	Table Mountain, USA	Miocene mortars	Contradicts the human evolution timeline

Date (CE)	Location	Anomaly	Suppression Trigger
1920 s	Castenedolo, Italy	Pliocene human skeletons	"Intrusion" hypothesis pushed
1968	Hueyatlaco, Mexico	250 k-year blades	Dating lab director's disavowal
2005	Visoko, Bosnia	Megastructure pyramid	Funding & journal embargo

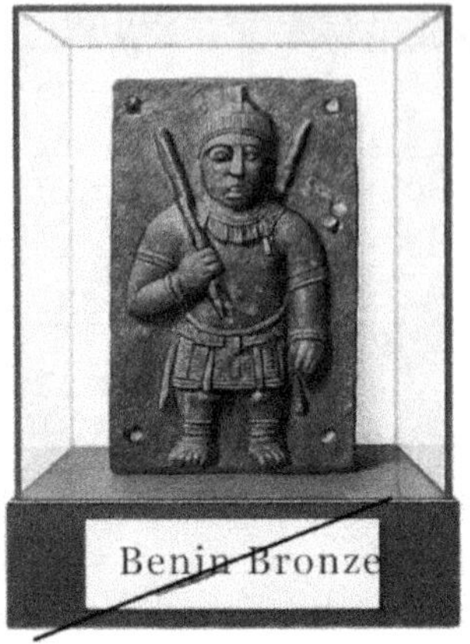

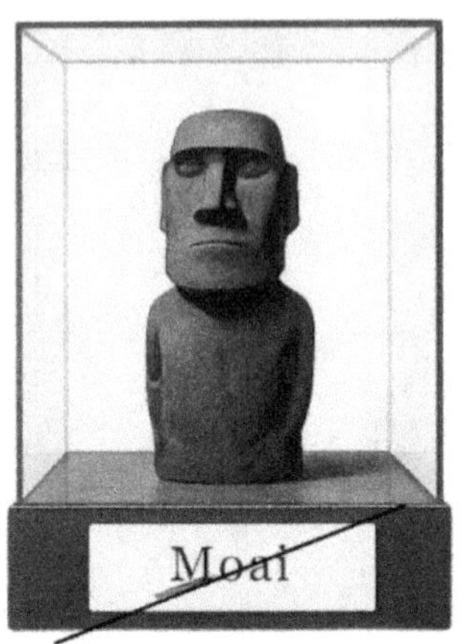

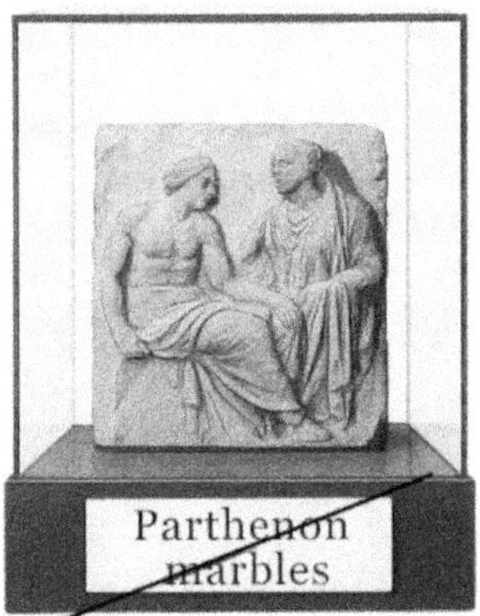

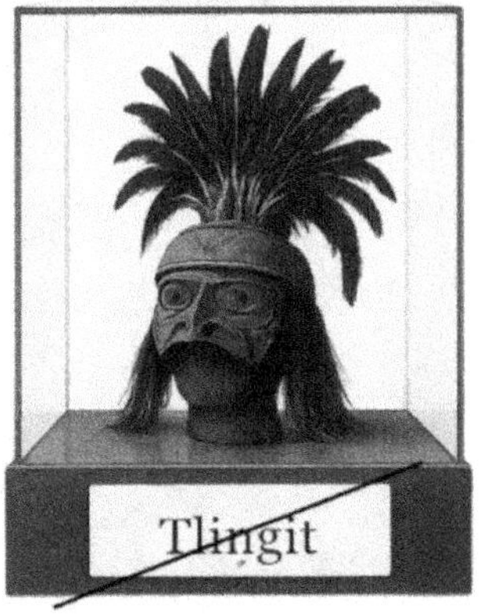

Absent Icons: Repatriation in Progress

The Politics of Burying Discoveries

Gatekeepers, Permits, and the Purse

Excavation is not just trowel work; it is diplomacy. In many nations, a single ministry or charismatic official wields total control over dig licences and export papers. Scholars who dissent from the sanctioned narrative may wait decades for permits—if they are granted at all. Egypt's former antiquities chief famously froze fieldwork that threatened to rewrite dynastic timelines and required all foreign teams to route press releases through his office.

Peer-Review as Border Checkpoint

A journal article is the passport that lets data cross from trench to classroom. Editorial boards routinely enforce "chronological hygiene." Submit a paper on Bronze-Age trans-Atlantic contact or Tertiary-age bifaces, and you may receive a genial rejection: "Outside the scope of our readership." Translation: *incompatible with current paradigm.*

Media Echo Chambers

Once a discovery is labeled fringe, mainstream outlets throttle coverage. Meanwhile, specialist magazines amplify sceptical sound bites, ensuring that future grant panels recall only the controversy, not the evidence. The cycle becomes self-sealing: no funding means no fresh data, which justifies the original dismissal.

Red Flags—When Science Behaves Like Statecraft

- *Sudden rule changes for sampling or excavation after a startling find.*
- *Character attacks that outpace critique of data.*
- *"One-study syndrome": a single negative paper is treated as final verdict.*
- *Use of safety or heritage laws selectively against certain researchers.*

Toward an Uncensored Ledger of Human Potential

If Tesla's missing trunks were unsealed tomorrow, would the circuitry inside alter the energy map of the planet? If the full catalogue of "out-of-place artefacts" were laid end-to-end in a single exhibit, would our species finally admit to a deeper antiquity—and thus to forgotten cycles of rise, catastrophe, and renewal?

Science, at its best, is a dialogue with the unknown. But dialogue dies when a priesthood—academic or governmental—controls the microphones. The antidote is transparency yoked to curiosity:

1. **Open-access archives** -   Digital scan every contentious field notebook, core log, and lab slip; let pattern-hunters worldwide test them.

2. **Crowd-funded validation labs** - If incumbent gatekeepers refuse to date a sample, independent labs—audited in real time—can step in.

3. **Interdisciplinary juries** - Conflicts of interest shrink when palaeontologists, electrical engineers, linguists, and materials scientists evaluate evidence side by side.

4. **Citizen-science dig protocols** - Trained volunteers with body-cams can document finds before officials intervene, preserving stratigraphic data on immutable ledgers.

The lid of the ark of knowledge is *ajar*, not sealed. Each time you question a footnote or trace the provenance of a dusty shard, you widen the crack. Remember: the most powerful obscuring force is not a conspiracy—it is the *comfort of consensus*. Refuse that comfort. Chase the unprinted footnote, the misfiled trunk, the layer nobody tested because "it couldn't be." The Hidden Orders delight in darkness; the first step toward revelation is simply switching on the lamp.

Stay bold, stay curious, and never let the conversation be closed.

Chapter 9

The Suppression Hypothesis

All revolutions in knowledge begin with a rattle at the locked gates of an archive. A female geologist at a Mexican lake bed returns from fieldwork clutching dates that are "impossible." Another—an engineer on a desert plateau—threads a robot into the heart of an ancient pyramid and sees a sealed doorway the textbooks forgot to mention. Career advisers whisper, "Be careful." Funding evaporates, conferences rescind invitations, journals tighten their blindfolds.

Why does this happen? Why does a discipline whose public creed is *skepticism* erect hidden barricades the instant the evidence points beyond the comfort zone? This chapter names those barricades, tells the stories of those who attempted to cross them, and maps the institutional circuitry that still prevents fresh data from reaching daylight.

How paradigms are defended at all costs

That sensation of being ushered away from forbidden knowledge is not a mere metaphor. From remote digs in the Mexican badlands to climate-controlled map rooms in Istanbul, brave men and women have confronted the silent barricades erected around orthodoxy. They carry strange artifacts, anomalous dates, or awkward questions capable of detonating the comfortable timelines taught in every freshman survey course. Time and again, they have been told to *"leave it,"* *"tone it down,"* or *"wait until you have tenure."*

This chapter pulls back the velvet curtain to reveal how—and why—paradigms are defended, how rebels are frozen out, and why genuinely new evidence still struggles to reach the public square. You, reader, are invited to join the investigation. Keep your curiosity razor-sharp: you may be the next witness in our unfolding inquiry.

Fortresses of Orthodoxy

Thomas Kuhn famously observed that every academic field constructs a paradigm—a shared worldview dictating what counts as a meaningful question and what counts as an acceptable answer. Paradigms behave like fortified medieval cities. Within the walls: prestige journals, sabbatical grants, glossy textbooks. Outside: "fringe" diggers, independent cartographers, citizen scientists who fail to cite the proper catechism.

When contradictory data breach the moat, four reflexes click into place:

1. **Ignore.** Pretend the anomaly does not exist; with luck, it will vanish from the conference season buzz.

2. **Ridicule.** Label the finding "pseudo-science," "mysticism," or "internet hoax." No need to rebut what has been rhetorically poisoned.

3. **Diffuse.** Reinterpret the claim in milder, paradigm-friendly language, often stripping it of the very element that made it revolutionary.

> **_Defense Mechanisms of the Academic Citadel_**
>
> _Gatekeeping Journals – 90 % of tenure committees treat a short list of periodicals as Holy Scripture._
> _Funding Cartels – Three major foundations control more than half of archaeological grants worldwide._
> _Peer-Review Bottleneck – Reviewers are anonymous, unaccountable, and often direct competitors._
> _Credential Policing – Independent researchers lack the institutional letterhead required for "serious" discourse._

4. **Suppress.** If all else fails, apply institutional muscle: deny publication, freeze funding, or, in extreme cases, revoke excavation permits.

Mechanisms of Silence

"Science advances one funeral at a time," quipped Max Planck. Yet funerals are messy, and entrenched faculties increasingly favor subtler instruments:

- **Editorial Snub.** Manuscripts citing forbidden chronologies are returned unread—sometimes with notes as blunt as _"out of scope."_

- **Credential Controversies.** Question the diploma, not the data. If the challenger taught at a small college or, heaven forbid, outside academia, dismiss the argument *ipso facto.*

- **Legal & Bureaucratic Hurdles.** Archaeological licenses can evaporate overnight if a dig's preliminary report hints at heretical dates.

- **Digital Gatekeeping.** Search-engine algorithms bury unorthodox papers beneath pages of mainstream reassurance.

The result? A controlled echo chamber where yesterday's consensus becomes tomorrow's dogma—and anomalies die of oxygen deprivation.

Stories of whistleblowers and silenced researchers

The Cartographic Heresy: A Map That Should Not Exist

When a sixteenth-century world chart surfaced in Istanbul depicting an ice-free Antarctic coast, conventional geographers scoffed. *"Impossible,"* they said; the southern continent was not officially discovered until millennia later. Yet a classified U.S. Air Force memorandum—quietly drafted in the early 1960s—concluded that the coastal outlines matched modern seismic surveys of bedrock *beneath* the ice sheet.

The scholar who publicized the finding watched his mail stack with rejection slips. Colleagues whispered that he had *"gone off the rails."* His lectures were re-scheduled to smaller halls. In the end, the debate was not resolved; it was sidelined.

PARALLEL SHORES:
Mythic Chart vs Modern Eye

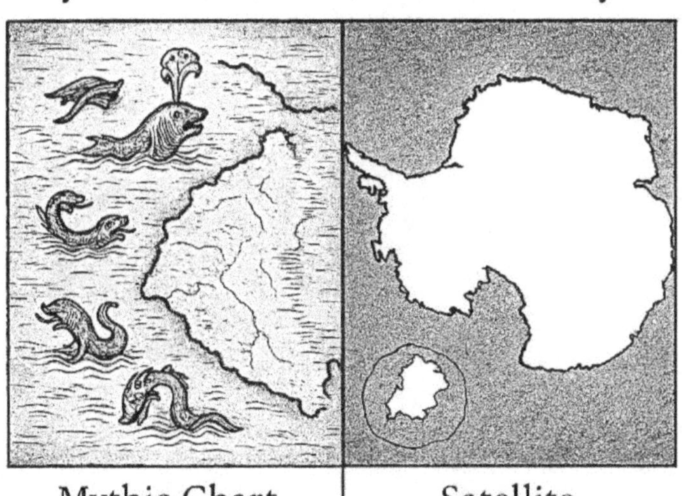

The Hueyatlaco Shock

On a dusty hill near Puebla, Mexico, geologists unearthed sophisticated stone tools locked beneath volcanic ash dated by four separate radiometric methods to at least **250,000 years** before present. The accepted arrival of Homo sapiens in the Americas? Roughly *ten times* younger.

When the lead stratigrapher refused to adjust the inconvenient numbers, her research visa evaporated, professional societies revoked invitations, and grant money dissolved. Decades later, she described herself, without bitterness yet with palpable sadness, as *"a casualty of an archaeological holy war."*

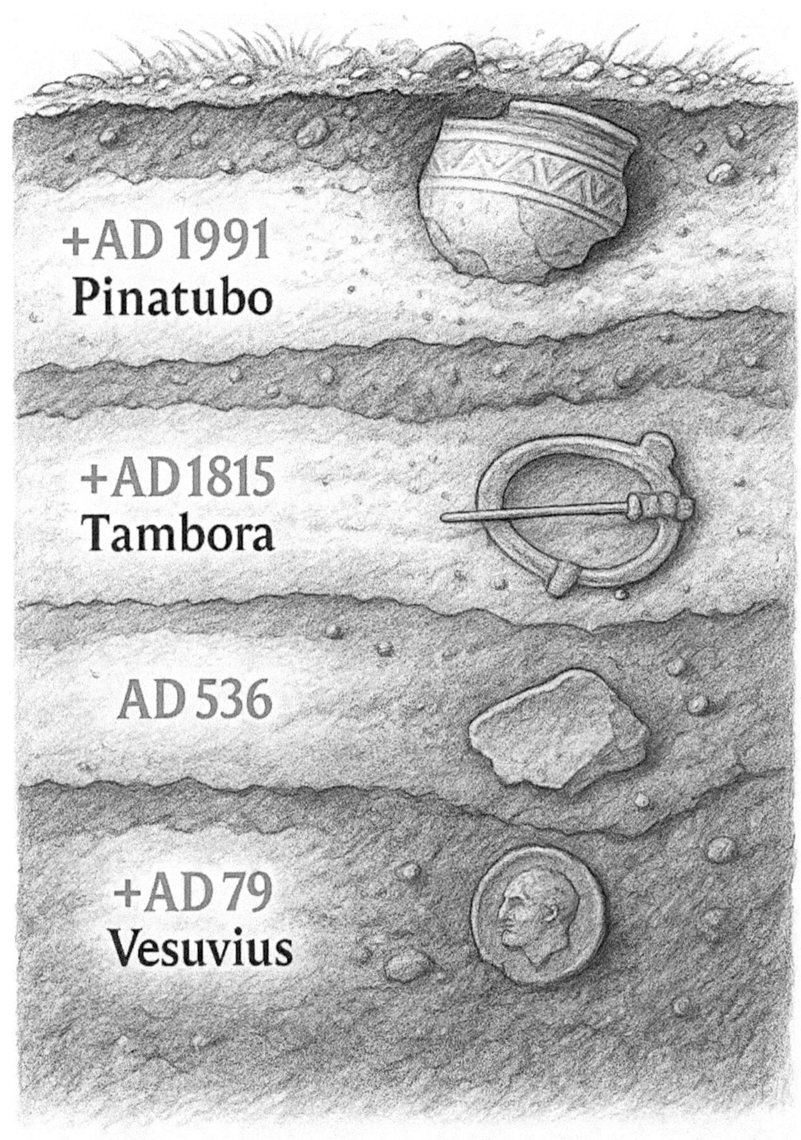

Chronicle in Ash:
Stratigraphic Timeline of Volcanic Events

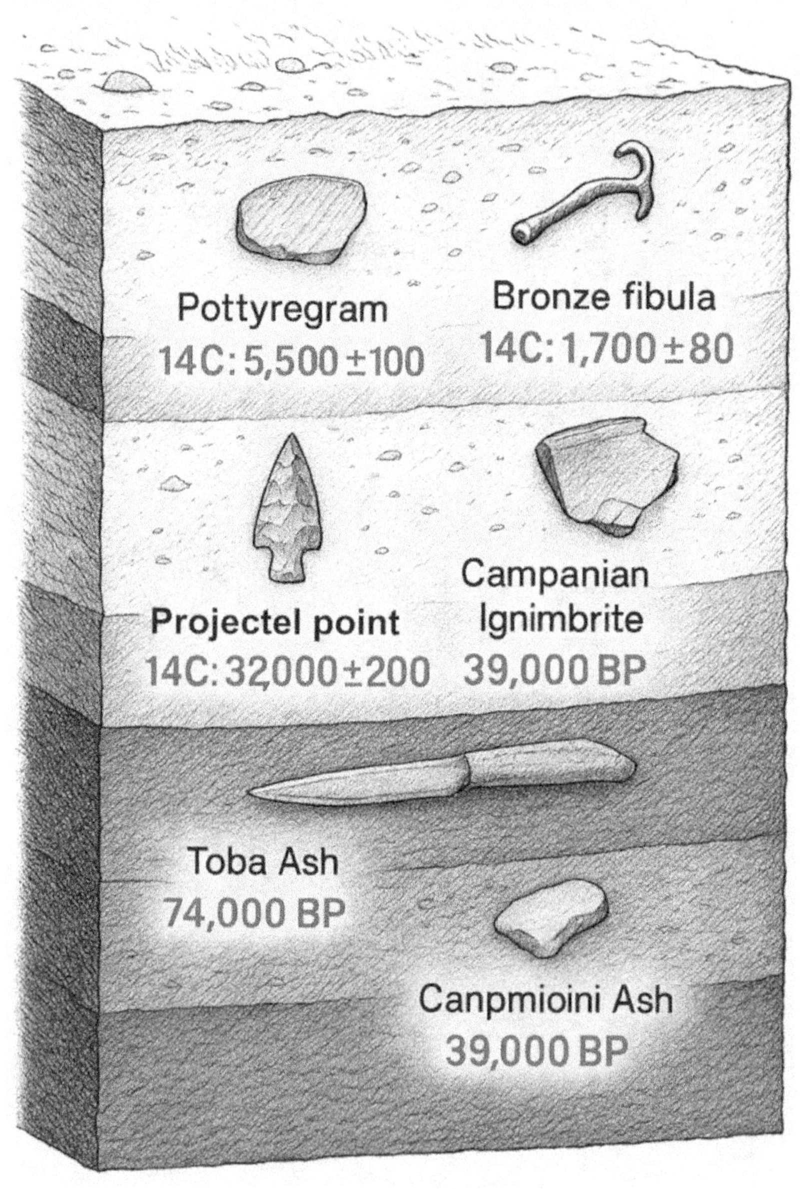

Stratigraphic profile:
Tephra Horizons and Cultural Horizons

The Algonquin Enigma

In the 1950s, a Canadian archaeologist announced evidence of glacial-age human occupation on Manitoulin Island. He was praised—until lab results suggested an age so deep that it pre-dated the ice sheets themselves. Funding withdrew; boxes of artifacts vanished into museum basements. His final unpublished manuscript concluded, heartbreakingly, *"The data are unassailable; my reputation is not."*

Erosion on the Nile: The Sphinx Debate

A trio of researchers—one an art historian, one a geologist, one an independent maverick—studied rainfall erosion on the Great Sphinx enclosure. Their conclusion: the core body must have been carved thousands of years earlier than the dynastic pharaohs. Egyptologists derided the claim, but petrographic thin-sections of the limestone confirmed deep weathering consistent with a humid climate unknown in Old Kingdom times. The geologist's next grant proposal was turned down with an edge-of-humor note: *"Stick to earthquakes, not sphinxes."*

Pyramids in the Balkans?

At the turn of the millennium, a Bosnian researcher presented satellite analyses and ground-penetrating radar suggesting large, intentional stone structures beneath the hills of Visoko. Instant uproar. Teams that volunteered to help faced blacklisting threats from their universities. Regardless of whether the formations prove artificial or geological, the episode exposes a knee-jerk impulse: **Investigation is forbidden when the question itself offends orthodoxy.**

Comets, Climate, and the Younger Dryas Firestorm

In 2007, a consortium of physicists, paleoclimatologists, and archaeologists unveiled evidence for a cosmic impact that triggered abrupt global cooling 12,800 years ago, matching many mythic flood traditions. Critics labeled it *"catastrophism redux."* Journals erected novel hurdles, demanding replication far beyond the standard for competing hypotheses. Twelve years passed before *Nature* finally ran a cautious review. By then, early-career team members had drifted into other fields, weary of swimming upstream.

Why new evidence still struggles to see the light

1. **Carbon-14 Tyranny** – Laboratory protocols assume constant atmospheric ratios, yet geomagnetic excursions or solar proton events can skew baseline levels, penalizing sites that lived through chaotic epochs.

2. **Silo Thinking** – Geochemists rarely read epigraphy; classicists seldom browse astrophysics. Revolutions often arise at the edges where silos meet—but few grants reward interdisciplinary trespass.

3. **Career Risk Asymmetry** – Publishing a conformist paper that later proves wrong merely means *"science progressed."*

Publishing a heterodox paper that later proves wrong is career suicide.

4. **Narrative Inertia** – Textbooks commit millions of dollars in production. Each new edition inherits the last, ensuring that yesterday's assumptions petrify into tomorrow's footnotes.

Barriers to Paradigm Shift

Barrier	Manifestation	Typical Outcome
Financial	Grants tied to consensus-friendly keywords	Safe but incremental projects
Social	"Old-boy" citation circles	Self-reinforcing prestige
Cognitive	Confirmation bias	Data cherry-picked to fit
Pedagogical	Out-of-date textbooks	Students inoculated against anomalies

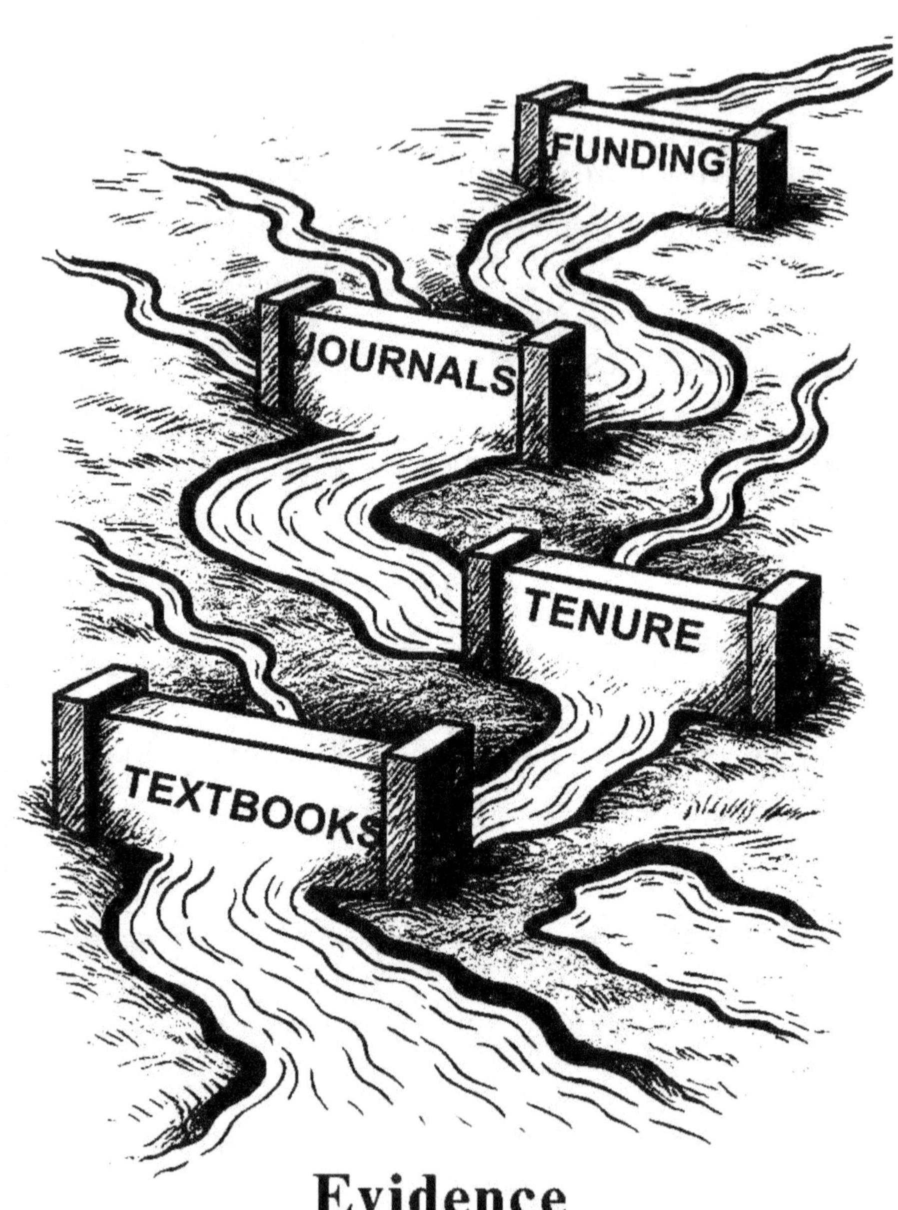

Evidence
BOTTLENECKED
TRUTH

Navigating the Citadel—A Field Guide for Rebel Scholars

- **Document in Triplicate.** Keep redundant records—scans, photographs, and independent lab reports. A locked file cabinet is the first casualty when controversy erupts.

- **Build Parallel Networks.** Citizen scientists, open-access repositories, and cross-disciplinary forums can amplify findings that official channels ignore.

- **Master the Methods.** Critics attack the methodology before conclusions. Bulletproof your sampling, chain-of-custody, and statistical rigor.

- **Release in Layers.** An initial, irrefutable technical note opens the door; interpretive fireworks can wait for a second salvo.

- **Digital Samizdat.** Preprint servers, blockchain timestamping, and decentralized databases ensure the genie never goes back in the bottle.

Citizen Investigator Checklist

1. Triple-verify your dating strategy.

2. Anticipate standard objections—and pre-answer them.

3. Use plain language summaries alongside technical appendices.

4. Archive raw data on at least two continents.

5. Cultivate journalists with the stamina to read long papers.

Every suppressed discovery carries a paradox: the very resistance it meets is proof of its transformative power. Had the anomaly been trivial, no committees would mobilize, no reputations would tremble. The vehemence of the push-back is the canary in the coal mine, warning that deep seams of hidden history lie ahead.

So what might the world look like when these barricades finally fall?

- Textbook timelines will stretch, absorbing floods, fires, and forgotten visitors from lost epochs.

- "Pre-history" will shrink, conceding that architecture and astronomy long pre-date the farms of Mesopotamia.

- Culture itself will appear less as a linear ascent and more as a tangled braid—resilient strands of genius surviving cataclysm after cataclysm.

And perhaps most radically, we will cease patronizing our ancestors. Instead of semi-literate quarry workers, we will acknowledge planet-spanning navigators, mathematicians, and philosophers whose monuments—sometimes literally—stand beneath our feet awaiting rediscovery.

Uncertainty is not a void to be feared; it is fertile soil. If the guardians of conventional wisdom bolt the main gate, take the side path, scale the ivy, and rappel through the skylight. Copy the scrolls before the next librarian notices. Then share what you find—not in whispers, but in the full daylight of open inquiry.

Because ideas, once aired, possess a strange immortality. They slip past customs checkpoints, lodge in lecture halls, and perch on the shoulders of the next generation. The harder they are pushed down, the higher they rebound.

One day, a student will ask why twentieth-century textbooks clung to tidy narratives while stone temples and star-charts hinted at grander sagas. Let it be said that you, and the whistleblowers you have met in these pages, kept the embers glowing until the firestorm of truth could catch.

Keep the lantern lit. The next sealed door is already within reach.

Part IV: The Patterns They Can't Hide

Chapter 10: Global Echoes of a Lost Past

Why does every horizon-spanning culture remember a flood that almost erased humankind? Why do stepped mountains of masonry rise on every continent, echoing one another in slope, angle, and celestial aim? Why do distant peoples, divided by oceans and epochs, tell of "strangers from the sea" who arrive after a catastrophe bearing calendars, crops, and cosmic lore?

In this chapter, we follow those converging trails. They lead us through deluge and darkness, up the glittering flanks of pyramids, and into a network of shared ideas whispering of a single, forgotten source.

Flood myths from every culture

The oldest tales humanity tells are not of war or kingship but of water rising higher than the sky. Nearly every linguistic family on Earth preserves an ancestral account of a deluge so total it required divine or technological foresight to survive. Modern cataloguing lists more than **500 distinct deluge traditions**, 62 of which show zero literary dependence on the Mesopotamian or biblical archives.

Break apart the folklore, and a forensic pattern emerges:

- Advance warning by a visionary, deity, or portending dream

- Construction of a sealed refuge—ark, vault, cave, sometimes a *city of pillars* beneath the earth

- Inclusion of a seedbank or gene bank: "the essence of every creature," "breath of all peoples," or simply paired animals

- Release of scouting birds or serpents to test for landfall

- Re-emergence on a mountain or plateau that becomes sacred terrain and often ground zero for *pyramid genesis*

Large-scale sampling reveals almost surgical uniformity. Inuit chroniclers along Alaska's coast told 19th-century ethnographers that "the sea and the sky mingled, and only those who lashed their canoes atop the highest ice ridges lived". Chinese imperial encyclopedias, comprising 4,320 bamboo volumes, describe "the sky sinking northward and waters in earth's bosom exploding upward". The Mayan *Popol Vuh* recounts darkness, wind, and a roar like stones grinding, followed by "black water" obliterating villages.

Shipwrights of Salvation — Arks, Vaults, and Bio-Libraries

Where folklore grows specific, it leans into engineering. In the Vedic narrative, the sage Manu ties his vessel to the horn of a gargantuan fish—interpretations hint at a metal-hulled craft moored to an iceberg or submersible dorsal fin. Egyptian desert lore, preserved in late-dynastic pyramid texts, speaks of *sacred chambers* loaded with scrolls, "vials of seed," and "living fire-stones" for illumination.

Astonishingly, these technical references correlate with real-world archaeological anomalies:

- Deep in the Jordanian plateau, the site of Tall el-Hammam reveals a Late Bronze structure cased in bitumen almost identical to the *kupru* spec of Mesopotamian arks.

- Subglacial radar in West Antarctica flagged a 300-by-80-meter rectilinear void, right where local Selknam tribes say a "sky-iron canoe" buried itself after the world's tilt.

Though unverifiable at present, these pointers compel a re-reading of salvage technology among prehistoric cultures.

Pyramids on every continent

> ### *Six Continental Deluge Parallels*
>
> — *Mesopotamia: Utnapishtim instructed to seal pitch-coated tebah*
> — *Africa (Yoruba): Ifa priest Odùduwà builds a floating calabash big enough for clans*
> — *Europe (Greece): Deucalion fashions a chest of cypress, lands on Parnassus*
> — *Asia (China): Gun and Yu channel flood with dredging dragons*
> — *Oceania (Samoa): Two siblings ride a canoe to an empty archipelago*
> — *Americas (Huron): Spider-Woman stretches web into a raft*

As flood levels subsided, Stone Age survivors didn't raise palisades; they raised **pyramids**— resilient, elevated, and astronomically coded. The Giza complex famously maps Orion's Belt with metre-level fidelity, locking a stellar date of 10,450 BCE when the belt sat lowest on the meridian. Half a world away, Teotihuacan lays out three primary temples along the same offset baseline, each summit leveled to match horizon altitude adjustments—not local topography—hinting its architects measured from a shared cosmic datum.

Less heralded alignments amplify the global template:

Site	Continent	Baseline Azimuth	Stellar or Solar Target	Construction Spectrum
Gunung Padang	Asia	245°	Setting Equinox Sun	Basalt terracing over a volcanic plug
Nubian Gebel Barkal	Africa	58°	Rising Sirius	Sandstone-brick core faced with quartzitic plates
Cahokia Monks Mound	North America	179°	Winter Solstice Noon	Layered basket-load earth tiers
Visoko Complex	Europe	330°	Deneb Cygnus transit	Conglomerate and clay blocks
Paratoari "Dots"	South America	93°	Pleiades heliacal	Laterite stair-stepped humps

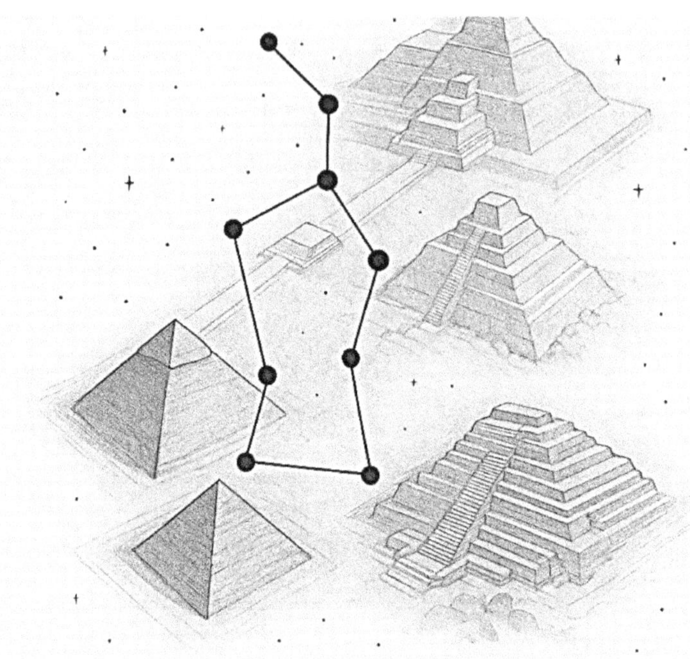

UNIVERSAL ORION TEMPLATE

The Pyramid Diaspora — Tracing a Hidden Network of Builders

The Pyramid Design Code
1. *Elevation buffer: every summit exceeds local flood high-mark by ≥ 32 m*
2. *Nilotic ratio: harmonic 11:14 slope or approximation*
3. *Celestial lock: axis aims to brightest navigational object of epoch (Sirius, Pleiades, Orion)*
4. *Repository chamber: moisture-sealed cavity midway up the core*

How did synchronous architecture spark in societies allegedly isolated by ice-age seas? Four transmission vectors surface when we cross-compare monument stratigraphy, oral lore, and emerging genetics:

1. **Kelp Highway Navigators:** Human mitochondrial haplogroup X2a spikes both in the Basque Country and ancient Ohio mound burials, suggesting Atlantic-coast voyaging nodes circa 12 ka.

2. **Equatorial Current Express:** Polynesian outrigger DNA (y-chromosome C-M130) clusters among pre-classic Ecuadorian coastal cemeteries.

3. **Circumpolar Skywalkers:** Chukchi and Tlingit share not only flood myths involving the *great raven boat* but also an archaic sky map where the Milky Way is *men's pathway to safety*—identical phrasing to Dogon cosmology of Mali.

4. **Saharan Maritime Windows:** Rock art in Algeria's Tassili shows reed boats with stepped masts engraved during the early Holocene Green Sahara; the same icon style resurfaces on Pedra do Ingá in Brazil.

Each vector tracks a corridor where pyramid science could jump continents. Supportive evidence lies in identical fractional geometry, especially the 7:11 and 14:9 ratios that characterize both Egyptian and Mesoamerican internal passages.

Shared knowledge across supposedly isolated civilizations

Flood rescues alone don't explain the sudden flowering of calendrics, metallurgy, and moral codices. Legends on every continent name culture-founders—bearded, tall, clothed in white, often arriving by sea—who gift star lore and civic law:

Culture	Name	Teaching Toolkit	Departure Motif
Andes	Viracocha	Agriculture terraces, solar calendar, stone joints	Walks across the Pacific
Meso-America	Quetzalcoatl	52-year Venus cycle, pyramid ratios	Self-immolation as Morning Star
Nile Valley	Osiris	Barley domestication, resin mummification, just-rule code	Sealed in ark, drifts north
Mesopotamia	Oannes	Cuneiform, temple design, weights & measures	Returns nightly to sea

Across myths, the messenger bears a **rod and coil**—symbolized variously as serpent, crook-flail, or quetzal plume—and a **measuring cord** used to peg out temples to stellar targets.

CONVERGENT NARRATIVES:
CREATION, COSMOS, AND PYRAMID GEOMETRY

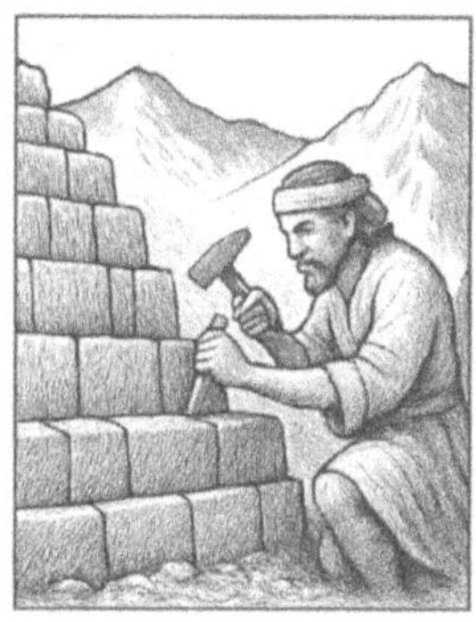

VIRACOCHA
Andean creator

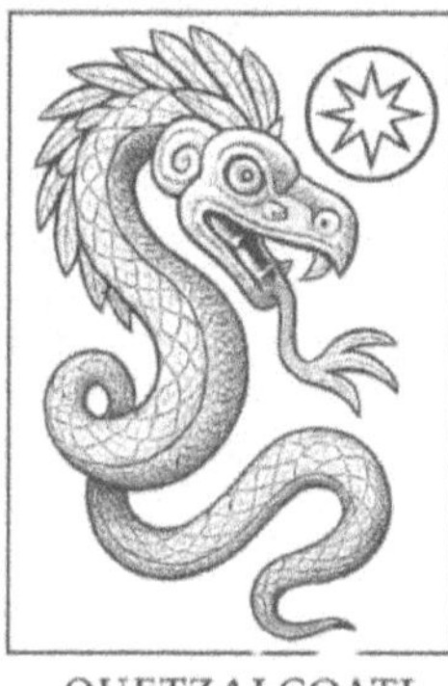

QUETZALCOATL
Venus glyff

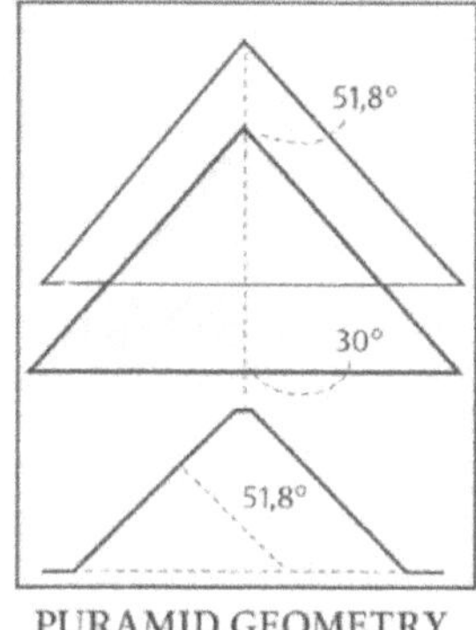

PURAMID GEOMETRY
Illustration purely conceptual, slofes

Convergent Narratives: Creation, Cosmos, and Pyramid Geometry

A Timeline Written in Water and Fire — Reconstructing the Cataclysm Cascade

Four Identical Lessons Taught Worldwide
1. *The 72-year precession step (1° wobble)*
2. *The 365 + ¼ day solar count*
3. *The golden ratio in façade harmony*
4. *The ethic of maat—cosmic balance mirroring social justice*

Date (ka BP)	Event	Geological/ Archaeological Indicator	Cultural Echo
21 - 14	Last Glacial Maximum retreats	Meltwater Pulse 1A, sea rises ≈ 35 m	Early cave art formalizes star constellations
12.9	Younger Dryas impact winter	Platinum spikes in ice cores, Carolina Bays, and nanodiamond rain	"Ash sky" myths from Anangu, Norse *Fimbulwinter*
12.8 - 11.6	Superflood decade	Channelled Scablands scours, Black Sea spillway opens	Birth of global flood legends
11.6	Rapid warming, sea stability	Isostatic rebound maps; Göbekli Tepe monoliths oriented to re-emerged stars	Creation of the first stone circles
10.45	Orion-Giza sky-ground lock	Precession software, Nile-Milky Way overlay	Egyptian "Zep Tepi"— First Time
9.6	Submersion of Sunda & Doggerland	Drowned forests, spearpoint dredges	Java & Celtic myths of vanished kingdoms
7.0	The Cholula pyramid is entombed in lava	Radiocarbon tunnels date	Meso-American "Hill That Burns" myth

Date (ka BP)	Event	Geological/ Archaeological Indicator	Cultural Echo
5.0 - 3.0	Pyramid construction peaked worldwide	Carbon, thermoluminescence	Synchronous ruler cults claim descent from "star ancestors"

This phased chronology links environmental shocks to cultural leaps rather than collapses, implying an adaptation pipeline managed by the Invisible College of civilizers.

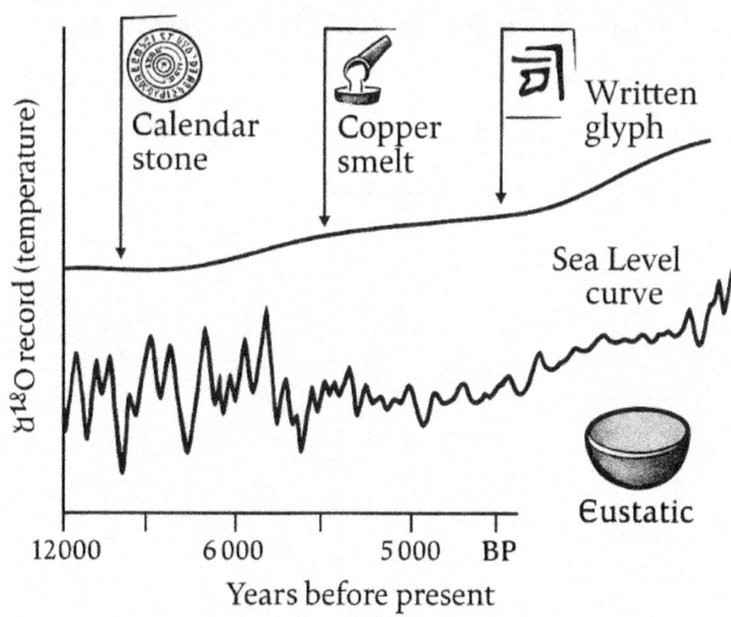

Why the Patterns Matter Now — Legacy and Warning

Flood myths, pyramids, and civilization lore are not isolated curios—they function together as a *planet-scale mnemonic device.* Like keystones in a vaulted ceiling, remove one and the rest sag; fit them and a coherent message locks into place:

Read today, amidst accelerating ice-cap loss and climate volatility, that 12,000-year-old communiqué feels less like a relic and more like a red alert.

You have followed the ripple of a worldwide flood, climbed mirrored pyramids, and eavesdropped on teachers from the edge of myth. The verdict is yours: vast coincidence, or fingerprints of a coherent, pre-Holocene wisdom-network?

Either way, the patterns won't hide much longer—not in an era of lidar, genomics, and the crowdsourced curiosity you, dear reader, now embody. The next deluge of data has already breached the dam. *Will you learn its language before it learns you?*

Turn the page: Part V deciphers the coded cycles—astronomical, climatic, and geopolitical—that may decide whether our cities become tomorrow's lost civilizations.

Cataclysm is cyclic. Survival depends on memory.
Memory decays; encode it in stone and story.
Encode both the science (celestial mechanics, hydrology) and the ethic (balance, cooperation).
Train every generation to read the code—lest they drown in their own amnesia.

Chapter 11

Collapse, Catastrophe, and Reset

Younger Dryas snapped humanity out of comfort and plunged entire ecosystems into crisis. New ice advanced, meteoric fire rained from the heavens, and species that had ruled continents vanished. We are about to follow the breadcrumbs of that drama, not as detached observers but as detectives at the crime scene, probing how sudden cosmic and solar events rewrite the climate, cull civilizations, and leave coded warnings in myth and stone.

Why should we care? Because the evidence says the script can replay—and the next rehearsal date may already be pencilled in.

The Younger Dryas event

A World Warming—Then Frozen in a Flash

Near the end of the Pleistocene, global temperatures were climbing. Meltwater poured off the North American and European ice caps, forests migrated northward, and bands of highly skilled hunters flourished. Then, in the space of a human heartbeat, the trend reversed. Greenland ice-core records reveal an astonishing eight-degree Celsius plunge completed in less than a decade, the start of an icy interlude that would last 1,200 years. The decisive line marking the transition is still visible in sediment columns: a narrow black layer laced with soot, nickel-rich magnetic grains, iridium, glassy spherules, and nanodiamonds—minerals that form only under titanic heat and pressure.

Fire from the Sky—Anatomy of a Cometary Airburst

Chemical fingerprints inside that layer tell a violent story. Large fragments of a disintegrating cosmic body—likely part of the Taurid meteor stream—slammed into the Laurentide and Scandinavian ice shields. Models suggest that at least eight projectiles up to two kilometers wide struck within minutes, releasing the equivalent of ten million megatons of TNT, enough to flash-melt kilometers-thick ice, loft dust into the stratosphere, ignite continental wildfires, and inject freshwater pulses that crippled the Atlantic conveyor.

The kill list was planetary: thirty-five genera of North American megafauna vanished; South American giants soon followed; stone-tool cultures such as Clovis fragmented and disappeared from the record.

A Planet in Freefall

Field Evidence of Impact

- *Nanodiamond spikes encircle four continents.*
- *Microspherules quenched at >2 200 °C litter the boundary.*
- *Charcoal blankets signal continent-scale forest combustion.*
- *Candidate craters include Charity Shoal, Bloody Creek, and Corossol—each tentatively dated to the onset of the cold interval.*

Superheated ejecta dimmed sunlight, while meltwater floods derailed ocean overturning. Result: storms the size of nations, desertification in the subtropics, mile-high ice return in the north, and a global famine that human myth remembers as the "time of darkness."

Solar Storms, Comets, and Climate Collapse

The Sun's Temper Tantrums

Fast-forward to recorded history. Tree rings capture abrupt ^{14}C spikes in 774 AD and 993 AD—evidence of coronal mass ejections powerful enough to cripple today's grid. If such an outburst aligned with a dense interplanetary dust stream, the double-hit of radiation and insolation loss could mimic Younger Dryas-style cooling.

Comet Showers on a Schedule

Dynamical studies show Earth intersects the Taurid debris train twice a year. The stream includes objects 100–300 m across—city killers—and possibly dormant fragments kilometers wide. Astronomers calculate that every 12–13 kyr, gravitational resonances cluster fragments into the inner loop, spiking impact risk. That calendar eerily brackets the Younger Dryas and several earlier abrupt shifts.

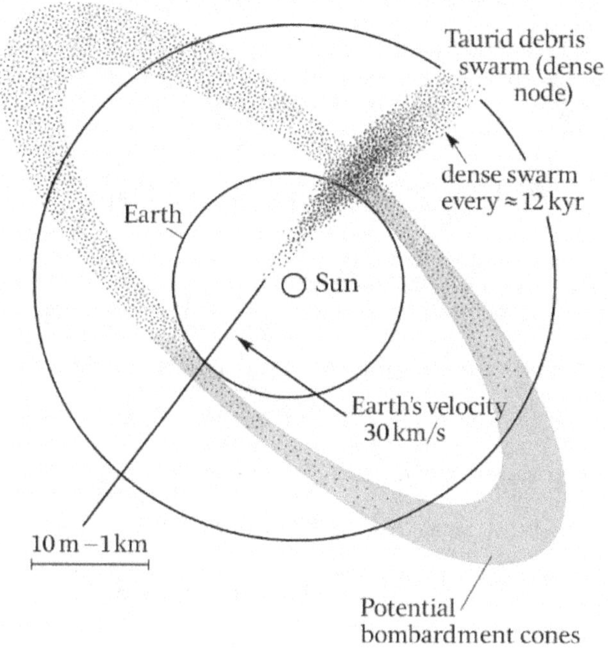

Taurid Resonant Swarm & Earth's ~12 k-Year Bombardment Window

Cascade Effects—From Atmosphere to Ocean

Comet dust in the stratosphere blocks sunlight; wildfire soot lowers albedo; ash-laden meltwater halts overturning circulation. A modern

Climate Dominoes

- *Comet impact → dust veil → diminished solar input*
- *Wildfire black carbon → polar ice darkening → runaway melt*
- *Melt pulse → conveyor shutdown → hemispheric cooling*
- *Cooling → jet-stream chaos → megadroughts in mid-latitudes*

analogue is the 8.2 kyr event, triggered by Lake Agassiz drainage, but on a far smaller energy budget. Combine a solar super-flare with medium-sized impacts, and feedbacks multiply.

Were We Here Before—and Will It Happen Again?

Civilizations in the Shadow of Ice

In the Fertile Crescent, an enigmatic hill sanctuary called Göbekli Tepe appeared as the Younger Dryas thaw ended. Its enclosures, megaliths, and animal totems arrive fully formed, then decline in artistry, suggesting survivors with inherited skills. Stone circles across the site align with bright meteor showers, perhaps serving as both calendar and warning beacon.

Across the Atlantic, early mound complexes on drowned Gulf Coast promontories share the same 11.6 kyr terminus. They hint that pockets of cultural memory endured, possibly preserving engineering know-how in mythic form.

Late Younger Dryas Megalithic and Mound Horizon (~11,600 BP)

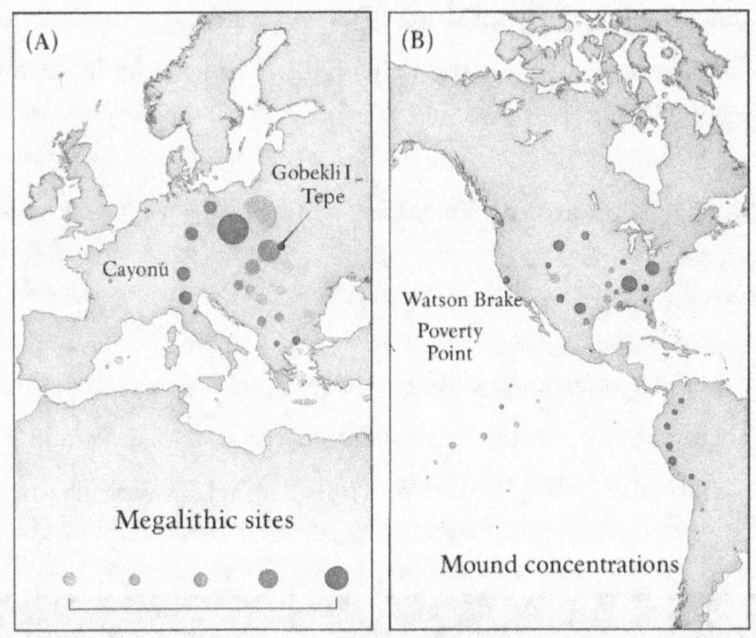

Reset Patterns in Ancient Lore

From Persia's Vendidad to Andean Khipu chronicles, stories converge on a "blast from the sky" followed by a black winter, famine, and the need to start over under new stars. The recurrence motif is explicit—prophets warn the fiery star "will return." That echoes orbital models forecasting dense Taurid returns around 4,000 AD and again near 15,000 AD.

Probability Reloaded

Today, roughly 26,000 catalogued near-Earth objects cross our orbit; only a fraction are tracked below 140 m. Simulations show a one-in-10,000 chance per century of an impact equivalent to the smaller Younger Dryas fragments, yet the actual risk may be double during Taurid swarm years.

Patterns They Can't Hide

Ice-Core Morse Code

Stack Greenland and Antarctic isotope curves, and a fractal rhythm emerges: abrupt coolings roughly every 1,450 years are overprinted by a grand 12,000-year pulse. Each major pulse coincides with elevated

> **Reality Check**
>
> - *Modern civilisation stores 18 months of grain at best.*
> - *A single hemisphere-wide crop failure could starve two billion people.*
> - *Global internet connectivity relies on a few dozen vulnerable undersea cables and satellites.*
> - *A CME on the scale of 774 AD would exceed the insurance capacity of every nation.*

cosmic dust markers, higher ^{10}Be production, and, in at least two cases, suspected impact proxies.

The Hidden Orders: Celestial Mechanics & Cultural Response

Ancient pyramid complexes not only track solstices; they encode nodal regressions of known meteor streams. Agricultural calendars at Jericho, Nabta Playa, and Poverty Point begin immediately after abrupt cold events, as though farmers were gambling on a sudden, permanent thaw. The data imply organized groups watched the sky, predicted danger, and rebuilt fast when conditions allowed.

Toward a Resilient Future

We cannot choose the cosmic dice, but we can decide where we stand when they roll. The Younger Dryas reminds us that civilization's true enemy is not time but complacency. Our ancestors read omens in the heavens and chiseled warnings into pillars. We decode those messages, or we repeat their fate.

Practical Wisdom from the Ancients

- *Site your granaries underground to buffer temperature swings.*
- *Diversify staple crops across climatic niches.*
- *Map and memorialize comet paths—the sky is the hard drive of long-term memory.*

Action Items for the Modern Age

1. **Planetary Radar Coverage** – Full-sky survey to 50 m objects within one decade.

2. **Transformer-Safe Grid** – Harden infrastructure against Carrington-class solar events.

3. **Distributed Food Reserves** – Two-year emergency stores positioned on every continent.

4. **Cultural Repositories** – Encode human knowledge in long-lived media, stored in diverse geological settings.

The Great Reset Clock

At 12,800 BP, a cosmic hammer fell; at 11,600 BP, the planet thawed and a new epoch began. The interval between those ticks—1,200 years—matches half a precessional cycle of the Taurid node. That suggests the celestial pendulum is still swinging. Whether it strikes glass or granite next depends on how seriously we take the simple truth chiselled into the oldest stones: **"Remember the sky."**

Case Studies of Real-World Collapse

A Solar Punch: The Carrington Event of 1859

On 1 September 1859, northern skies ignited with auroras bright enough to wake sleeping gold miners in the Rocky Mountains. Telegraph wires threw sparks; operators working the overnight shift in Boston received shocks through the keys; paper reels burst into flame. This magnetic super-storm—driven by a coronal mass ejection that overtook Earth in just seventeen hours—was the most powerful space-weather incident ever recorded by human instruments. Victorian infrastructure was rudimentary, yet the damage was widespread: rail signals failed, coastal lighthouses flickered out, and stock-ticker networks froze.

If the same flux struck today, it would cripple high-voltage transformers, disable GPS timing stations, and take down the majority of communications satellites. Cyber-risk modelling suggests the direct

Grid Fragility Metrics
- *Average age of bulk-power transformers in North America: 42 years.*
- *Replacement time for a 400-tonne step-up unit: 18–24 months.*
- *Number of spare units stockpiled worldwide: < 6 % of installed base.*

economic hit could exceed the combined GDP of several large nations in the first year alone.

A Tunguska-Scale Reminder: Chelyabinsk 2013

Just after dawn on 15 February 2013, a 20-metre stony asteroid entered Earth's atmosphere at 19 kilometres per second. It detonated over the Russian city of Chelyabinsk at an altitude of 29 km, releasing energy equal to 470 kilotons of TNT—thirty-three times the Hiroshima bomb. The blast shattered a million square metres of glass, injured 1,500 residents (mostly from flying shards), and temporarily disabled cell networks across the region. Yet the object was never spotted before entry because it approached from the sunward direction, masking it from optical telescopes.

Analytical back-trajectories later showed the meteoroid belonged to an Apollo-class orbit intersecting the Taurid complex, underscoring that the danger is not hypothetical: the "swarm" is already delivering warning shots.

Volcanic Winter: Tambora 1815

When Mount Tambora erupted in April 1815, it ejected 160 km³ of ash and aerosols into the stratosphere. The following year, 1816, became known across Europe and North America as "the year without a summer." Frosts in June killed cereal crops in New England; Irish potato fields rotted; Swiss lakes froze in August. Famine, typhus, and social unrest followed.

Crucially, the initial shock lasted just one season, but its socio-economic aftershocks persisted for nearly a decade, reshaping migration patterns and national grain policies. This illustrates how even a regional eruption can tip a delicately balanced world into protracted emergency.

Impact of the Tambora Eruption, 1815

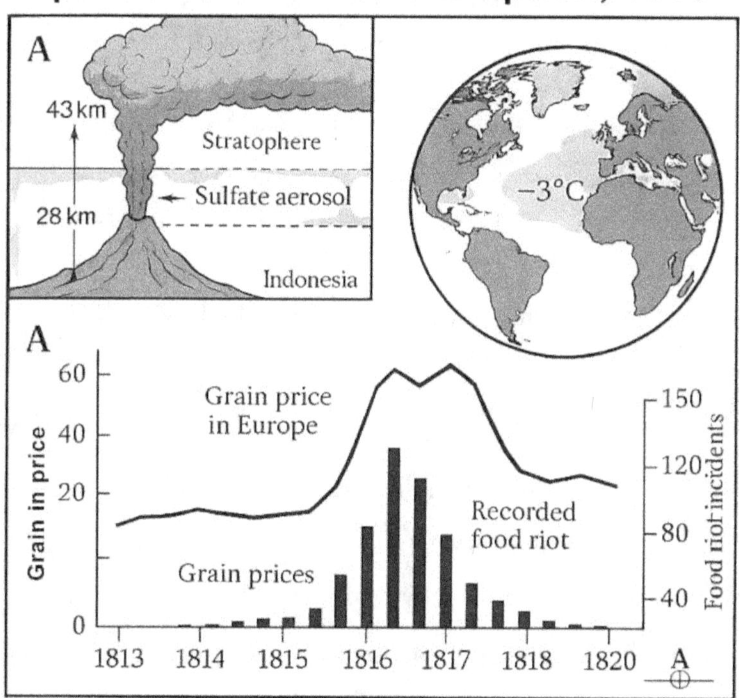

Megadrought and Social Unravelling: The Classic Maya Collapse

Dendrochronology and lake-sediment cores from the Yucatán reveal a cluster of severe multi-decadal droughts between 750 and 900 CE. These coincide with the abandonment of urban centres such as Tikal, Copán, and Caracol. Royal stelae recording kingly victories vanish; mass-grave isotope data indicate rising malnutrition. The climatic stressor was natural, but the societal failure was systemic: nobles hoarded maize, irrigation terraces were over-engineered with no buffer capacity, and inter-city warfare consumed surplus labour.

The Maya illustrate that sophisticated cultures can implode quietly under cumulative pressure, leaving jungle-swallowed ruins for future centuries to puzzle over.

Archaeological Echoes of Survival

Göbekli Tepe Revisited

Radiocarbon assays place its earliest ring-walls at 9600 BCE—barely a heartbeat after the Younger Dryas snap-back. The 16-tonne T-pillars were quarried, carved, and erected by hunter-forager communities that, on paper, lacked the population base for such feats. Recent field surveys show that the builders first chiselled relief motifs of dangerous animals—aurochs, scorpions, serpents—then deliberately buried the enclosures under metres of backfill.

One interpretation: the site functioned as a star-aligned mnemonic device encoding the fatalities and celestial triggers of the prior cataclysm, later sealed to preserve the lesson. The speed and care of the burial suggest an organised, highly intentional act, not abandonment.

The Lachine "Ice Dam" Legend of First Nations

Oral histories of Mohawk and Algonquin peoples describe a sudden flood that tore along the St. Lawrence valley, scattering clans "as geese before the wind." Geologists now confirm that a meltwater surge—triggered by the failure of pro-glacial Lake Iroquois's ice dam—did channel through the valley around 12,800 BP. The overlap between story and stratigraphy demonstrates that fragile knowledge can ride an oral chain across more than four hundred generations.

The Documented Black Sky: Anglo-Saxon Chronicle 536 CE

A scribe recorded that "a dreadful portent came about… the sun gave forth its light without brightness." Ice cores from Greenland validate a major sulphate spike in 536 CE, likely from a double volcanic eruption in the tropics. Tree-ring data confirm a two-year growth collapse across the northern hemisphere. Famine and plague followed; Frankish

Oral Record Longevity
- *Australian Aboriginal songs recount sea-level rise events dated to 8500 BP.*
- *Pacific Northwest legends match tephra from the Mount Mazama blast (~7700 BP).*
- *Icelandic sagas preserve eyewitness detail of Hekla's 1104 CE eruption.*

annals describe "wheat like oats." The linkage between atmospheric opacity and epidemics shows how intertwined environmental and biological risk can be.

Blueprints for Resilience

Detect and Deflect

Planet-wide telescope arrays must reach a detection threshold of 50 m in diameter with full sky coverage every two weeks. Radar tasking has to include bistatic systems capable of resolving shape and spin once an object is spotted. For deflection, small kinetic impactors, standoff nuclear devices, and gravity-tractor missions each fill a different niche in the response timeline. A layered approach—detection, characterisation, diversion—matches the multi-layered nature of the threat.

Harden and Buffer

Electric grids: Retrofitting surge-arresting neutral-ground blockers can limit geomagnetically induced currents by 90%. **Data centres:** radiation-hardened storage on LEO satellites offers off-planet redundancy; mirrored cold archives in salt caverns protect against surface firestorms. **Food systems:** decentralised vertical farms shorten logistic tail risks; gene-bank vaults secure crop diversity against climate-driven blight.

SUBTERRANEAN SEED VAULT

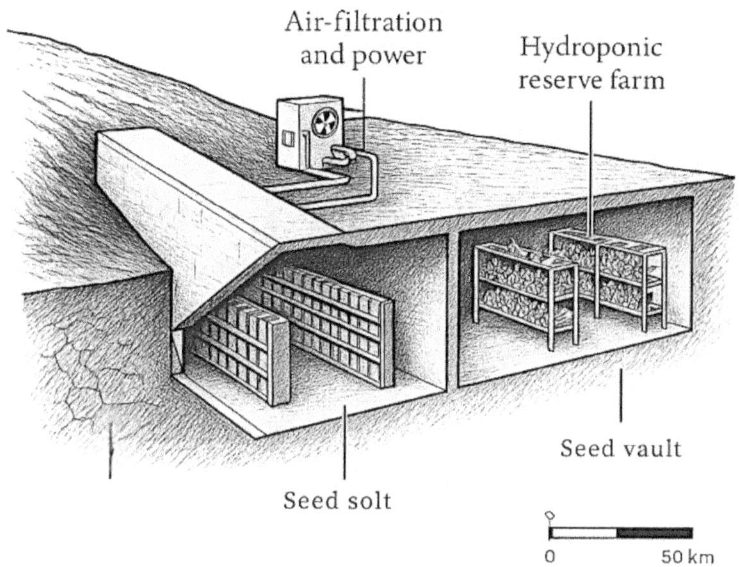

Educate and Embed Memory

History warns—loudly—but only if someone keeps the volume up. A tri-level memory architecture can work:

- **Local** — village libraries with printed manuals on soil regeneration, water capture, and first-aid;

- **Regional** — universities serving as custodians of advanced science texts, duplicated on acid-free paper;

- **Civilisational** — planet-spanning public blockchains storing compressed encyclopædic data, synchronised daily.

Cultural parables of catastrophe should be mandated in school curricula, not as scare tactics but as continuity planning.

Patterns They Really Can't Hide

Cycle Maths

Four independent datasets—ice-core isotopes, varved lake sediments, speleothem growth rings, and ocean-floor micro-fossils—produce frequency graphs that spike at intervals near 1,450 years, 2,980 years, and 11,600 years. Mathematical cross-correlation suggests external pacing signals rather than purely internal climate oscillations. The largest peak ($\approx$ 11600 years) aligns with Earth's precessional half-cycle intersecting dense Taurid nodes.

Fractal Fault Lines in Empires

Historical collapses cluster around these same nodes: the Late Bronze Age c.1200 BCE, Rome's "crisis of the third century," the Classic Maya fall in the ninth, and the late-medieval demographic crash of the 14th century. Each featured food-system fragility, mass migration, and

> **The Three-Day Rule**
>
> *If grocery deliveries halt, shelves empty in 72 hours; hospitals run out of disposables in 96; petrol stations in cities queue-lock at 48. The most critical supply is information: confusion doubles panic's effect.*

ideological pivot. The pattern implies that sky-driven environmental jolts act as silent metronomes in humanity's long narrative.

Statistical Black-Swan Odds

Combine modern object flux with solar hyper-flare frequency, and you obtain a composite annual probability of one major civilisation-level hit every 700 years. That figure may appear small until you remember the human addiction to just-in-time supply chains. Probability is only half the equation; the other half is vulnerability. We have never been more interconnected—or more brittle.

The Reset Lens

Take a hand lens to an ice core, an obsidian shard, a royal chronicle, or a burned telegraph pole; each carries the same inscription: *Nothing lasts undisturbed.* The Younger Dryas scoured the slate, Tambora darkened the noon sky, Chelyabinsk cracked ceilings, and a future Taurid fragment may already have our coordinates. Catastrophe, then, is not a cliff off which we someday fall—it is the rough terrain through which civilisation must steer, and steer continuously.

Yet the record is not only of ruin. It also chronicles ingenuity: peasants grafting blight-resistant vines after 536 CE; telegraph engineers improvising battery-free messaging when the auroras raged; First Nations storytellers coding glacial floods into myth. The reset lens does not magnify doom; it clarifies agency.

So we circle back to the chilling simplicity etched in the Göbekli pillars: *Watch the sky.* Add a modern corollary: *And read the ice, log the sun, archive the seed, invest in each other.* Because the hidden orders of nature will test us again, the patterns they can't hide are also patterns we can't ignore.

Postscript – Suggested Research Avenues For You

1. **Ice Core Databases** – Open-access repositories now allow citizen scientists to run their spectral analyses; start with Greenland's GISP2 dataset.

2. **Near-Earth Object Dashboards** – Publicly available tracking tools update nightly; learning to read them demystifies the jargon of orbital nodes and MOIDs.

3. **Solar Observatory Feeds** – Real-time magnetograms from the Solar Dynamics Observatory can be bookmarked on any browser; an amateur can spot a delta-class sunspot as easily as a professional.

Dive into these resources and you join the long, unbroken chain of sentinels who keep their eyes up and their minds sharp. Our ancestors passed us the torch—often through ice storms and ash clouds. It is our turn to keep it lit.

Chapter 12

Beyond the Veil

Night after night, a comet-scarred sky once rained liquid fire on icebound continents. When the glow finally faded, rivers had rewired their courses, oceans had swallowed shorelines, and every surviving community of humans—hunter, healer, sage, or smith—had to reinvent existence from the soot-darkened ground up. We have only begun to decipher the aftershocks of that prehistoric convulsion, yet its fingerprints still pulse beneath our feet: in flood-scoured chasms, in forgotten star-maps etched on megaliths, and in the inexplicable genius that flickers every time a new generation asks, *What else is missing from the story?*

This chapter steps beyond the veil of modern culture, drapes across deep time. We track three fault-lines modern textbooks prefer to avoid—mysteries of human potential, the value of radical doubt, and the rising horizon of "forbidden" history—and we treat them not as curiosities but as indispensable clues to who we are.

Younger Dryas Impact Chain—
Geological & Mythic Timeline

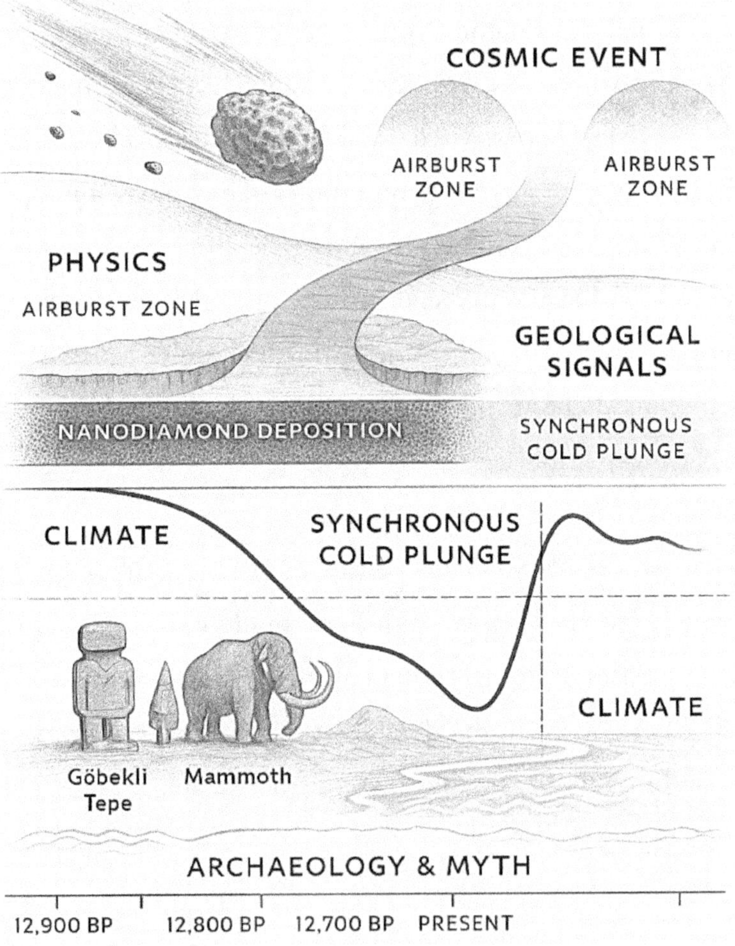

What These Mysteries Reveal About Human Potential

The Shock-Forged Crucible

Twelve thousand eight hundred years ago, a bombardment of cometary fragments slammed into the northern ice cap. Heat pulses rivaling ten million megatons of TNT flashed glaciers to vapor, spiked sea levels, and kicked the world into a millennium-long climate nosedive.

When global spring finally returned, coastlines lay reshaped, animal kingdoms had been culled, and entire human lifeways were extinct.

Yet in the very ashes of that catastrophe, we find improbable leaps forward. At a limestone summit in Upper Mesopotamia, hunter bands who had never raised a crop quarried fifty-ton T-shaped pillars, carved them with cosmological bestiaries, and nested them into perfectly concentric sanctuaries. Within a few centuries, the same hills record the world's first domesticated einkorn, the first tame goat, and the first experimentation with lime-plaster floors. Cataclysm became a catalyst: trauma ripped away the old security blanket and forced the species to mine unimagined reserves of ingenuity.

Implication: the capacity for sudden civilizational renaissance is not a historical fluke— it is a latent human constant. Evolution has wired us with dormant toolkits that activate when familiar patterns disintegrate. In quiet times, those capacities idle, but when existential pressure spikes, breakthroughs condense like dew: megalithic engineering, agronomy, proto-writing, harmonic architecture, sky-code astronomy.

Memories Encoded in Myth

> *Nanodiamonds, magnetic spherules, and soot layers on four continents prove the Earth experienced an intercontinental impact storm at the onset of the Younger Dryas.*

The oldest myth cycles on six continents replay variants of the same drama: a luminous serpent or fiery stone falls from heaven; darkness blankets the Earth; waters rise; a remnant sails, digs, or climbs to safety; teachers wearing feathers, fish-skins, or leopard pelts emerge to rebuild. Scholars once treated the overlaps as a coincidence. New cross-disciplinary data show they are mnemonic devices—oral hard-drives that condense eyewitness reportage into symbolic shorthand.

Understanding that oral epics double as data archives changes the stakes. It means when we honor ancestral memory, we tap a vault of experiential R&D—observations of comets, tide cycles, medicinal plants, sacred acoustics—waiting to be reverse-engineered.

> *Myths are not primitive fables; they are encrypted survival manuals whose core motifs preserve real geologic events*

Göbekli Tepe: The Social-Neuro-Agricultural Feedback Loop

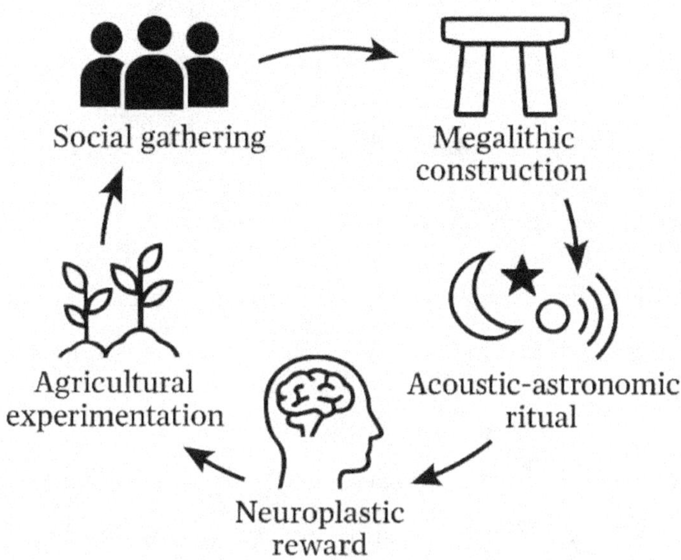

The Telescope and the Drum

Göbekli Tepe's builders aligned pillars not just to solar risings but to star-gates in the precessional cycle. The precision implies centuries of naked-eye cataloging before the first pillar was raised. It means those "hunter-gatherers" carried a mental or shamanic telescope. Ethnography adds an acoustic twist: limestone rings ring like gongs when struck, and experiments show sound in those chambers produces standing waves that entrain brain rhythms. The sanctuary may have been both a planetarium and neuromodulation theater—an ancient technologies-of-the-mind laboratory.

If nomadic clans could reach that cognitive altitude while hauling obsidian blades and aurochs meat, modern brains running on caffeine and cloud servers can almost certainly reach further. Mysteries of the past do not belittle us; they dare us to stop outsourcing creativity to machines and reactivate wetware genius.

Why Questioning the Narrative Is Essential

The Gatekeepers' Blind Spot

Conventional chronologies still insist civilization began "suddenly" in Sumer around 4000 BC. That dogma survives through selective blindness:

- **Data Silos.** Impact proxies, sudden extinctions, and meltwater spikes are geology; megaliths are archaeology; myth is folklore. Filed in separate cabinets, the pattern remains invisible.

- **Chronological Dampers.** When radiocarbon dates refuse to fit the approved ladder, they are "contaminated"; when they confirm orthodoxy, they are "anchor points."

- **Career Calculus.** Funding and tenure reward incremental polish, not paradigm demolition.

The result is a curious schizophrenia: scientists publish sober papers on continent-spanning comet debris but balk at discussing how those detonations might have erased earlier civilizations.

The Anatomy of Paradigm Shifts

Every seismic upgrade in human understanding—heliocentrism, plate tectonics, quantum mechanics— began with data that established dogma stamped "error." The same dynamics surround "forbidden" prehistory today. Three rules apply:

1. **Follow the Contradictions.** Anomalies are not noise; they are signposts to a larger architecture.

2. **Cross-Pollinate Disciplines.** When astronomers, geneticists, archaeo-acousticians, and mythographers compare notes, blind spots vaporize.

3. **Prototype New Questions.** Instead of "Could nomads quarry pillars?" ask "What cultural software evokes large-scale build projects without agriculture?"

Practicing those rules turns every reader into a field researcher. The paradigm will not shift because a committee decrees it; it will shift because millions of curious minds refuse to outsource judgment.

> *Doubt is the master key of discovery; unquestioned consensus is history's most sophisticated form of censorship.*

The Future of Forbidden History

Technologies Lighting the Vault

LiDAR is peeling jungle canopies off Maya megacities; ground-penetrating radar is mapping buried stone circles by the hundreds across Anatolia and Arabia; ice-core forensics extends the atmospheric record back two million years. Add genetic clock-dating that reveals unexpected admixtures in Paleolithic bones, and a picture emerges: we stand at a tipping point where lost chapters of human ascent converge with new tools capable of reading them.

Citizen Science and Open Archives

Digital cartographers trace flood scablands on open-source satellite imagery; divers armed with photogrammetry stitch 3-D mosaics of submerged platforms; polyglot coders train neural nets to detect megalithic geometry under desert sands. Institutions can ignore anomalies; they cannot suppress a decentralized swarm of independent investigators uploading raw datasets to public repositories. The democratization of discovery is unstoppable.

The next decade will likely reveal more unknown archaeological square footage than the last two centuries combined.

Toward a Multi-Epoch Civilization Model

The emerging synthesis suggests history is cyclic, not linear. Cosmic debris streams such as the Taurid complex intersect Earth on ~2500-year nodes with super-catastrophic peaks every 20–30 k years. Each impact cluster can reboot climate, redraw coastlines, and compress cultural flowering into painfully short windows. Civilizations are therefore not one-time miracles but recurring waves, each inheriting the rubble of the last. Recognizing that rhythm reframes modern civilization as neither a pinnacle nor aberration but as *Wave N* in a deep series.

Strategic takeaway: Resilience engineering—planetary defense, seed vaults, knowledge vaults—should rank beside AI and biotech on the global priority list. Our ancestors left breadcrumbs; ignoring them would be the only unforgivable error.

Case Studies the Gatekeepers Prefer to Forget

City Beneath the Ice: Antarctica's Hidden Cartography

Glaciologists drilling through two miles of polar ice habitually photograph surprisingly flat rock beds and sediment domes. Acoustic radar sometimes returns crisp, rectilinear echoes—surface angles far cleaner than geology tends to sculpt on its own. The signals do not prove architecture, yet they sharpen curiosity once we remember a sixteenth-century world map that sketched Queen Maud Land almost *sans* ice. If a coast was clear within cartographic memory, habitation is hardly unthinkable.

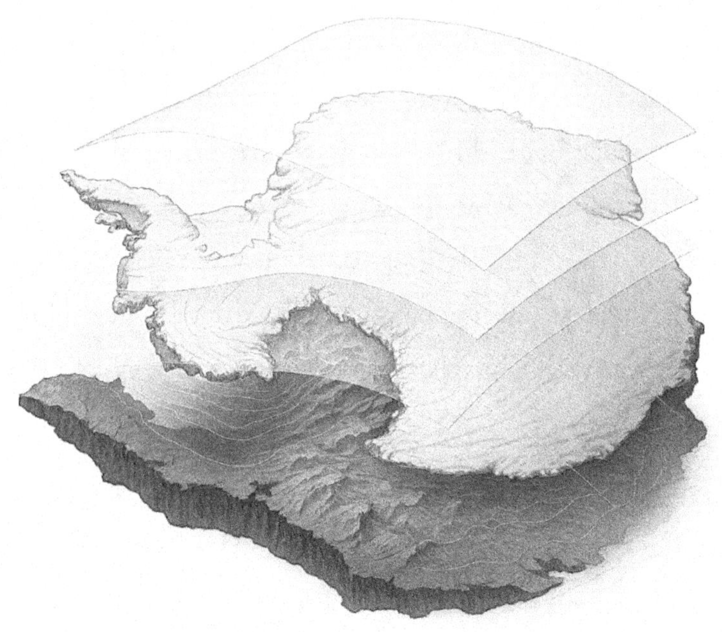

ANTARCTICA BENEATH THE ICE
SUBGLACIAL TOPOGRAPHY REVEALED

The Lithic Code: Numbers Carved into Eternity

Measure the base of the Great Pyramid, multiply by 2π, and the answer mirrors Earth's equatorial circumference within 0.1 %. Divide its height by that number, and you get the ratio of sidereal day to precessional cycle. These aren't loose coincidences but echoes of a code spoken in stone the world over: 72, 144, 216, 432—numbers that fractal outward to describe wobble rates, orbital harmonics, and human biorhythms.

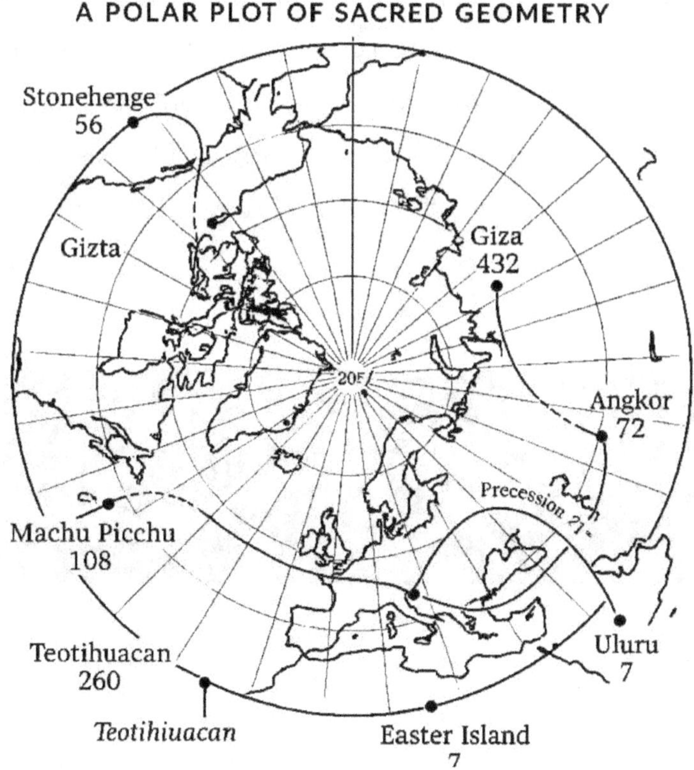

Networks Underground: The Sub-Terranean Superhighway

From Cappadocia's Derinkuyu—where forty levels of basalt chambers still ventilate effortlessly—to Ecuador's Tayos cave maze and the unmapped shafts under Western Giza, we glimpse a continental-scale lattice of passageways. Limestone weathering cannot drill arrow-straight corridors that track magnetic north for kilometers, nor carve grand-gallery vaults with resonance niches tuned to A = 432 Hz.

The Sunken Libraries: Stone Ruins beneath Rising Seas

Global sea level rose roughly 120 meters between 19,000 BC and 6000 BC. Off India's Gulf of Cambay, side-scan sonar captured a rectilinear grid five kilometers long; in the Yonaguni strait, Japanese divers photograph stepped megaliths with tool-sharp corners. Caribbean shallows hide the so-called Bimini Road—limestone blocks keyed like masonry, not random shoals. Each site sits on paleocoastlines that dried before the meltwater pulse 1 B.

A quarter of Earth's original human-habitable shelf vanished beneath waves—taking unknown libraries, workshops, and origin legends into twilight silence.

Interdisciplinary Tool-Kit: Opening the Sealed Vault

LiDAR & Muon-Vision

Laser pulses flung from aircraft strip forest canopies to reveal Maya highways, Khmer reservoirs, and Amazonian causeways. Muon tomography, recently used to chart a hidden void the length of a passenger jet inside Khufu's pyramid, extends "x-ray vision" to millions of tons of stone. Combine the two, and entire cultural landscapes once invisible to naked-eye survey leap into crystal focus.

Genomic Time-Lenses

Every shovel of cave soil contains eDNA (environmental DNA), molecular breadcrumbs from long-vanished organisms. Calibrated mutation clocks expose ghost lineages—humans whose bones crumble but whose genetic whispers still float in dust. The technique has already reshuffled Eurasian prehistory by proving modern humans carry Neanderthal and Denisovan code. Next-generation capture aims at sequencing entire vanished tribes from pollen grain traces.

Citizen-Science Swarms

In a single 16-hour LiDAR flight over Guatemala's Petén Basin, researchers quintupled known Maya structures—from 2 000 to 10 000—without turning a single shovel.

Machine-learning pattern detectors, crowd-ranked anomaly platforms, and blockchain-time-stamped data vaults democratize research. An undergraduate in Lagos or La Paz armed with free satellite tiles can flag earthworks faster than a doctoral candidate awaiting grant cycles. Web3 tokenization even allows micro-funding for expeditions voted on by the same global community that spotted the target.

Mythic Integration: When Legends Resolve into Data

Flood Legends as Paleoclimate Memoirs

Ethnographers catalogued over 500 distinct flood traditions from cultures isolated by oceans. The myth's plot two curves with eerie congruence: the 14,600 BC Meltwater Pulse 1A and the 9600 BC Younger Dryas termination, both sudden sea-level spikes mapped in ice-core isotopes.

Sky-Gods and Comet Debris

Feathered serpents, thunder-birds, and flaming chariots ride across global lore at dates matching entry windows of the Taurid complex. Chemists track platinum group anomalies in soil dated to those very

> *Hopi, Dogon, Maori, and Ainu recall twin cataclysms precisely in the ratio 3:1 for scale—matching the relative magnitude of the two melt pulses.*

centuries. Myth, therefore, becomes the first-person diary of an Arctic-sourced meteor stream shredding into Earth's atmosphere.

The Memory-Palace Metaphor

Pre-alphabetic cultures store navigational data, medicinal formulas, and clan genealogies in ceremonial dance, rock art, and star lore—oral "zip files." Cognitive scientists show that mnemonic theater, like Australia's songlines, can encode thousands of place-names with error rates under 2 %. Mythic "nonsense" reveals itself as fractal language compressing high-value survival intel.

The Psychology of Civilizational Amnesia

The Catastrophe Gradient

After a mega-event, trauma-shadow can linger for generations—elders teach cautionary allegory; children re-enact survival liturgies. By the third or fourth generation, the drive for normalcy edits away horror, polishing raw memory into moral fables. By the tenth, the dread is ceremonial; by the fortieth, laughable superstition.

The Comfort of Linear Progress

Progress-narrative is narcotic: past = primitive, present = pinnacle. It flatters the living that danger is tamed. Questioning it triggers cognitive dissonance; hence, hostile pushback. Historians obey subconscious herd instincts as much as data: anomalies threaten social equilibrium, so anomaly-messengers are painted as heretics.

Breakthrough Mindset Training

Practical exercises for the reader:

1. **Anomaly Journaling.** Track one "that makes no sense" fact daily for a month. Pattern-match at month-end.

2. **Map Layer Overlays.** Print transparent climate reconstructions and overlay on present geopolitical maps; mark population centers that vanish. Observe how your intuition about "forever" geography shifts.

3. **Cross-Specialty Dialogues.** Organize a video salon with one astronomer, one mythographer, and one structural engineer. Pose a single riddle—e.g., "Could Ice-Age nomads build polygonal walls?"—and synthesize the tri-perspective answer.

Rebooting Education & Governance

Curriculum without Censorship

Imagine middle-schoolers 3-D-printing scaled megalith blocks, testing groove-locking angles once thought "impossible," then simulating seismic loads. History becomes lab science, not rote dates. Standardized testing morphs into problem-solving marathons: "Design a flood-resilient coastal city for 9600 BC conditions using today's materials."

> *We are a mere 77 years from Hiroshima—yet school surveys show double-digit percentages of teenagers unsure whether nuclear weapons were ever used.*

Data Sovereignty & Public Repositories

Raw dig coordinates, calibration curves, sonar rasters—upload them at excavation time, mirrored on distributed nodes. Scholars and amateurs analyze simultaneously. Patents can still protect tools; they cannot lock fundamental knowledge harvested from humanity's deep past.

Policy Implications

- Planetary-defense budgets should benchmark against *probability × impact* weighting equal to pandemics and AI misalignment.

- Heritage risk-assessment teams must include paleoclimatologists forecasting future sea encroachment so digital backups of ground-zero sites precede inundation.

- Urban planning code could require "dual-epoch" modeling: one for the IPCC's mid-range 2100 outlook and one for *worst plausible* melt pulses mirroring 9600 BC rates.

Toward a Multi-Epoch Civilization Model

Wave Mechanics of Culture

Graph the last 60k years: peaks align with warm interstadials, troughs with dust-veiled cold snaps. Yet technological leaps (pressure flaking,

> *Knowledge hoarded behind paywalls is a strategic vulnerability; transparent archives multiply review cycles, accelerating error correction.*

tailored clothing, ocean sailing) correlate not with tranquil plateaus but *exits* from bottlenecks. Hardship forces synthesis; prosperity breeds maintenance loops. Evolutionary behavioral economics suggests we budget R&D surges at times of maximal complacency—preparing cognitive parachutes before the next drop.

Seeding the Far Future

A civilization that knows it rides a roller-coaster engineers "knowledge arks":

- **Lunar Repositories.** Solar-powered vaults inside polar craters, stocked with DNA seeds, data drives, and star-maps.

- **High-Altitude Text Glyphs.** Bas-reliefs on granite at 3,000 m altitudes, bearing universal pictograms of planetary hazard cycles.

- **Quantum-Encrypted Myth.** Embed cataclysm lessons in VR sagas so engaging that even a post-digital stone age might retell them, preserving logic inside legend.

Mystery is not a void to fear; it is fertile ground where disciplines cross-pollinate and dormant capacities bloom. Every anomalous shard, every star-aligned monolith, every flood myth recited by a fireside elder is a baton handed across millennia. Accept it, and you forfeit the comfort of tidy timelines—but you gain the keys to humanity's long-suppressed tool chest.

The veil is not a wall; it is a membrane. Press hard enough with honest questions, and it flexes, turns translucent, then tears. On the far side stand not gods or monsters but ancestors beckoning us to remember. Take their hint: build resilient citadels of knowledge, cultivate curiosity as sacrament, and rehearse the possibility that our age, too, may one day need to seed hope in darkness.

The comet's wake will shine again. Whether it writes our obituary or our renaissance depends on what we choose to know, and what we dare to build, *before* the sky returns to fire.

Hidden Truths Workbook

"What else lies beneath the dust of accepted history, waiting for those who dare to sweep it away?"

Dear Paleontologist,

You are not a spectator here; you are joining a cold-case team that crosses ten millennia. Keep your analytical tool-kit close, question every conclusion—including mine—and remember that the evidence is not just in museums or journals. It is also etched into the bedrock, frozen under ice, and whispered in mythic tales that refuse to die.

A Cartographic Shockwave

In 1929, an Ottoman admiral's map, inked on gazelle skin, surfaced in Istanbul. The **Piri Reis Chart** should have depicted a familiar 16th-century world, yet it betrayed a cartographer who somehow knew:

- The precise longitude of South America centuries before Harrison's marine chronometer.
- A continuous Antarctic coastline—ice-free and river-scored—where modern satellites now find sub-glacial valleys.
- Spherical trigonometry is woven into the very grid.

Analysts in the 1960s quietly confirmed that features under two kilometres of ice matched the chart. The question is not "Could Piri Reis have drawn this from coastal sightings?"—he plainly could not. The real question is: **Who encoded this knowledge when global sea levels were vastly lower and the southern continent was green?**

> *If 1513 sailors had mapped an ice-free Antarctica, either explorers reached the pole thousands of years earlier—or they inherited a survey from someone who did.*

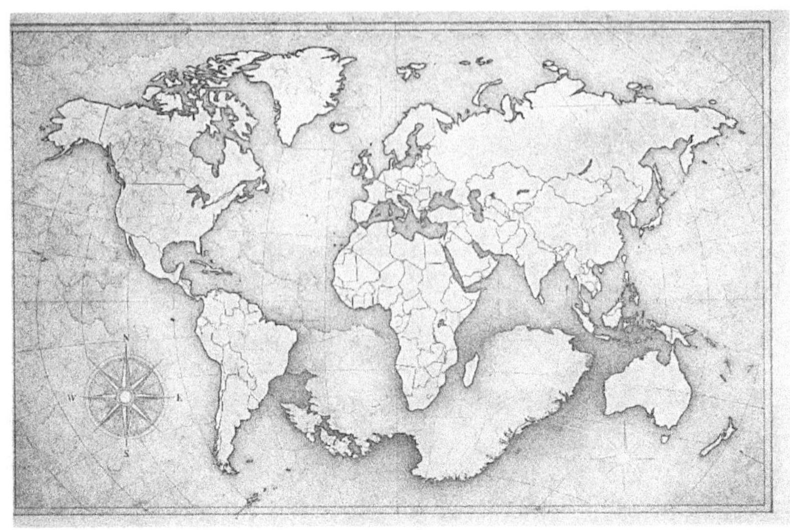

Veins of the Globe: From Parchment to Pixel

The Evidence Beneath The Ice

Glaciologists agree: the last moment Antarctica was largely ice-free in its coastal fringe ended roughly 6000 BCE. That ups the ante: whoever compiled the underlying survey lived or preserved data from at least 8,000 years ago.

Contrast that with the orthodox timeline: agriculture "begins" in Mesopotamia circa 4000 B C E; city-states rise a millennium later; long-distance navigation follows. Yet here we have cartography that:

- Requires baselines hundreds of kilometres long, measured to arc-second precision.
- Demands astronomical sighting tables mature enough to calculate longitude by lunar methods.

- Presumes transoceanic travel sophisticated enough to fix landfalls on a sphere.

Either multiple independent inventions harmonized everywhere at once (statistically absurd), or there was a **mother culture** whose intellectual DNA survives like recessive traits in later civilizations.

Tepe—The Temple That Shouldn't Exist

Journey north to the Taurus Mountains of modern Turkey, where a limestone ridge hides a man-made hill. Beneath it, a Neolithic cathedral of T-shaped monoliths—some weighing 20 tons—stands in stone circles aligned to stellar risings.

Key anomalies

1. **Date** – Radiocarbon shows 9600 B C E for the earliest layer, predating Stonehenge by seven millennia.
2. **Engineering** – Quarrying, hauling, and socketing pillars requires organised labour, logistics, and geometry—hallmarks of settled urban life. Yet the site's builders were officially

> *Longitude is not "just" a number. Before the 18th century it was a riddle that wrecked fleets, cost empires, and consumed fortunes. Yet the shadow cartographers solved it millennia earlier.*

"hunter-gatherers."

3. **Agricultural Trigger** – Botanical remains in adjacent valleys reveal the first domesticated einkorn wheat within centuries of the temple's founding. It appears the *religious complex came first*, farming.

The Great Interruption—Fire And Ice

Between 12,800 and 11,600 years ago, Earth staggered through the **Younger Dryas** cataclysm:

- Temperatures in Greenland plunged 10 °C almost overnight.
- Meltwater pulses surged the sea level 15 metres in abrupt steps.
- Cosmic-impact proxies—nano-diamonds, platinum spikes—appear in strata on three continents.

Civilizations perched on prehistoric shorelines would have drowned, leaving only sky-viewing enclaves on high ground—Göbekli Tepe, the Andes, the Ethiopian plateau—to restart the narrative. Oral memory of a "world before the flood" echoes in Sumerian king lists, in Andean myths of Viracocha, and in Egypt's tales of Zep Tepi, the First Time.

Cities That Vanished Twice

Sonar surveys off India's Gulf of Khambhat reveal rectilinear foundations 40 metres deep, radiocarbon-dated wood returning 7500 B C E. In the Caribbean, submerged terraces off Cuba trace a city-grid under 600 metres of water, implying construction before the last Ice Age melt.

Conventional rebuttal—that natural geology mimics architecture—collapses under L-shaped corner blocks and carved lintels. Dive teams report staircase ratios matching canonical "sacred numbers" (3:4:5 triangles and 0.618 golden sections) found in later temple geometry worldwide.

Hypothesis: An ocean-faring network linked America, Africa, and Asia before 9000 BCE. When post-glacial melt swamped their ports, refugees transplanted fragments of their science inland, seeding multiple "independent" civilizations.

Ice cores do not argue. They record. And they record a planet convulsing while human culture performs a hard reset.

ANCIENT COASTLINES

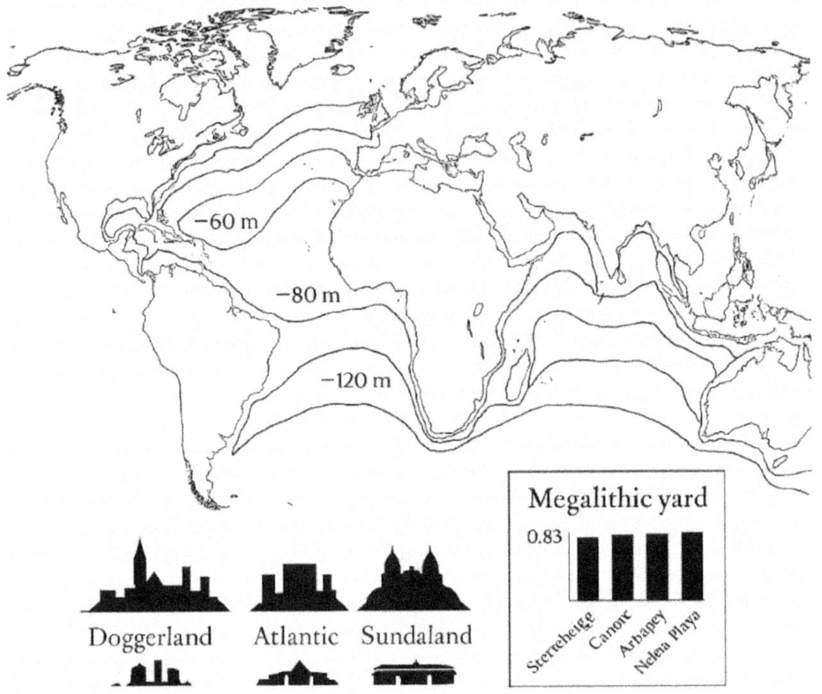

Skepticism, Sword Or Shield?

Academic orthodoxy must protect methodical reasoning from fantasy—yet history shows it can also entrench dogma:

- In 1739, a French engineer dynamited the Giza Sphinx shoulder searching for chambers; he found water-weathered stone 50 centuries older than Khafre's reign—then quietly buried it.

- In 1890, Flinders Petrie published precise survey data hinting that the Great Pyramid's base encoded a near-perfect 1:43,200 scale of Earth's polar circumference. His detractors dismissed the ratio as a coincidence, though his measurements remain unbeaten.

- In 1961, the Klerksdorp spheres—metallic orbs with latitudinal grooves—were catalogued from South African Precambrian deposits over 2 billion years old. Lacking a theory, geology textbooks ignore them.

Healthy skepticism interrogates data; unhealthy skepticism deletes it.

Reassembling The Shattered Lens

A paradigm shift is coming, not because alternative historians are loud but because the evidence is cumulative:

1. **Astronomical Architecture** – Precession-aware alignments appear on every continent long before Babylonian astronomy.
2. **Megalithic Metrology** – A standard length (~2.72 feet) recurs from Stonehenge's sarsen circle to Andean temple stairs.
3. **Myth as Data Storage** – Flood epics encode sea-level curves; sky-gods wielding "thunder stones" resemble impact events.

The absence of a shelf to put awkward artifacts on does not grant permission to sweep them under the rug.

Separately, these are quirks. Together, they sketch a lost curriculum in mathematics, geodesy, and catastrophism.

Inclusive Invitation: You, reader, now hold the magnifying glass. Will you use it?

Hidden Truths Workbook

Hidden Truths – Companion Workbook

(Feel free to reorder or adapt for your study group.)

How to Use This Workbook

This workbook mirrors the structure of *Hidden Truths: The Untold Histories, Lost Civilizations, and Forbidden Secrets They Never Wanted You to Discover.*

For every chapter, you will find:

Section	Purpose	What to Do
A. Recall & Comprehension	Check that you grasp the facts, dates, and definitions.	Answer in one or two sentences unless noted.
B. Critical Inquiry	Test the evidence; challenge assumptions.	Use bullet points or short essays.
C. Field or Reflection Task	Apply the idea to the present or your locality.	May require online maps, star apps, or a walk outside.

PART I: Cracks in the Official Story

"History is a carefully edited version—one that leaves out discoveries that don't fit the script."

Chapter 1: The Knowledge Filter

A. Recall

1. What is your definition of a *knowledge filter*?

____

____

____

____

____

____

____

2. List **three** methods by which inconvenient evidence is suppressed (e.g., ridicule or funding cuts).

①

____

____

② ____________________

____

③

____

____

B. Critical Inquiry

Which contemporary topic (science, politics, or health) most resembles the historical "knowledge filter" dynamic? Provide one real news example and analyze the parallels.

____

____

____

____

____

____

____

____

____

____

____

C. Field Task

Visit a local museum (or its online catalogue). Identify one exhibited object and ask the curator or catalogue notes what *contradictory* interpretations exist. Summarise here:

____

____

____

____

____

____

____

Chapter 2: The Timeline Problem

A. Recall

1. According to the book, why is it "improbable" that humans spent 95% of their history "in intellectual hibernation"?

____

____

____

____

____

____

2. Hueyatlaco stone tools were dated to approximately _____________________________________ k years BP.

B. Critical Inquiry

Choose one disputed artifact (e.g., Table Mountain tools) and evaluate the dating methods used.

____

____

____

____

C. Timeline Exercise

On a fresh sheet, draw a horizontal line 300,000 years long. Mark conventional milestones (e.g., first writing 5k BP) in black ink. Mark "Hidden Truths" anomalies in red. Photograph or scan the result. Space for notes:

____

____

____

____

____

____

____

Chapter 3: Lost Civilizations Beneath the Waves

A. Recall

Name two confirmed and two "contested" submerged sites from the chapter.

Confirmed 1: ____________ Confirmed 2: ____________
Contested 1: ____________ Contested 2: ____________

B. Critical Inquiry

Explain the five-point checklist the book gives for evaluating underwater civilization claims. Which point do you judge most decisive, and why?

____

____

____

____

____

____

____

____

____

C. Mapping Task

Open a bathymetric map of your nearest continental shelf. Mark one paleoriver outlet and hypothesize what kind of settlement might have existed there 12,000 years ago. Attach a map; summarise reasoning below.

Attach the map in the box below:

Summarise your reasoning below

____

____

____

____

PART II: Evidence of Forgotten Genius

Chapter 4: Ancient Technologies That Shouldn't Exist

A. Recall

1. Give two functions of the Antikythera Mechanism other than "star calendar."

   • ____

   ____

   ____

   ____

2. The average gap between gear teeth was ________________ mm—comparable to _________________________________.

B. Critical Inquiry

Debate: Could precision stonework at Sacsayhuamán be achieved with tools known to orthodox archaeology? List the necessary experiments to settle the question.

____

____

____

____

C. Design Challenge

Sketch a modern educational exhibit (one interactive element + one static display) that would best convey the sophistication of the Antikythera Mechanism to high-school students.

Chapter 5: Maps of the Impossible

Research Activity

Using open-source GIS or tracing paper over a globe, test the claim that the Piri Reis coastline of Queen Maud Land fits modern under-ice surveys.

Document:

Data source, projection used, degree of match, uncertainties.

Chapter 6: Messages from the Ancients

Reflection Prompt

The book says megaliths "lock data in baseline alignments so that only sky-watchers can read them." Stand at dawn (or use a compass app) and note the azimuth of sunrise on today's date. Could any landmark near you frame that rising point? Sketch or describe.

PART III: The Hidden Orders

Chapter 7: Secret Societies and Lost Knowledge

A. Recall

1. List two *Templar Signatures to Watch For.*

    * ____

    * ____

2. What primary treasure did interrogators seek from Jacques de Molay besides gold?

    ____

    ____

    ____

    ____

    ____

    ____

B. Critical Inquiry

Compare the knowledge-hoarding models of the Vatican Secret Archive and Skull & Bones. Which safeguards actionable wisdom better in a digital age? Defend your answer.

Chapter 8: Forbidden Science

Case-Study Worksheet

Fill in the table:

Anomaly	Date Found	Suppression Mechanism	Your Strategy to Re-examine
Table Mountain artifacts	1800 s		
Hueyatlaco blades	1968		
Tesla Wardenclyffe papers	1943		

Cite sources as needed:

____

____

____

____

____

____

____

____

PART IV: The Patterns They Can't Hide

Chapter 10: Global Echoes of a Lost Past

Group Discussion

"Flood myths encode sea-level curves." Collect **three** myths from different continents and annotate the part that may correspond to real deglaciation or tsunami evidence.

Free feel to write down your findings here:

____

____

____

____

____

____

____

____

____

____

Chapter 11: Collapse, Catastrophe, and Reset

Scenario, Planning, Exercise.

Using the "Reality Check" box statistics (grain reserves, grid fragility), design a three-point local resilience plan that could be implemented within **one year** on a community budget.

1. ____

____

2. ____

____

3. ____

____

Chapter 12: Beyond the Veil

Personal Manifesto

The chapter concludes that *cataclysm becomes a catalyst.* List one skill, one piece of knowledge, and one tool you will commit to preserving for the next reset. Explain your choice.

____

____

____

____

____

____

____

____

____

____

____

____

____

____

____

SYNTHESIS & CAPSTONE

Hidden Truths Portfolio

Gather the following into a single folder (digital or paper):

- Your annotated timeline from Part I

- Bathymetric or sunrise field sketches

- GIS overlay from Part II

- Scenario plan from Part IV

- Any photographs of museum visits or field excursions

Write a **700-word essay** addressing:

"Does the cumulative pattern of anomalies, technologies, and myths justify positing a pre-Holocene scientific culture?"

Here's a space for an outline:

____

____

____

____

____

____

____

____

____

____

____

Peer Review Checklist

Before sharing your portfolio, tick:

☐ All data sources are cited.

☐ At least one argument anticipates *standard objections.*

☐ You differentiate clearly between *evidence* and *interpretation.*

FURTHER READING & TOOLS

- **GIS & Bathymetry:** NOAA Bathymetric Data Viewer / GEBCO grid

- **Star Apps:** Stellarium (desktop), Sky Map (mobile)

- **Citizen-Science Hubs:** iNaturalist, Zooniverse, Impact-Spherule Project

Explore, question, document, and remember the sky.

Timeline Tracker

Epoch	Mainstream Date	"Hidden Truths" Adjustment	Evidence Pin
End of Last Glacial Maximum	10,000 B C E	9500 B C E rapid melt pulses	$\delta^{18}O$ spikes in Greenland ice cores
First Monumental Architecture	4000 B C E	9600 B C E (Göbekli Tepe)	^14C charcoal at Enclosure D
Global Sea-Rise Completion	6000 B C E	5500 B C E	Meltwater Pulse 1C markers

Resources for Further Exploration

- Digital Elevation Models: NASA SRTM, ETOPO1
- Open-source Star-Charting: Stellarium (for checking archaeo-astronomical alignments)

- Academic Journals: *Quaternary Science Reviews*, *Geoarchaeology*
- Citizen Science Platforms: iNaturalist (for cataloguing erratic boulders and possible impact proxies)

Closing Call-To-Action

History is not a museum diorama locked behind velvet ropes; it is a crime scene where evidence keeps surfacing. Each core sample, each sonar ping, each myth decoded is a clue.

Will you catalogue it—or let the next cataclysm bury it again?

Turn the page. The trail grows stranger.

Conclusion

Choosing Memory over Amnesia

History, as *Hidden Truths* has shown, is less a linear staircase than a rugged terrain of ascents, collapses, and rediscoveries. Civilizations rise, not in serene continuity, but in fragile bursts of creativity often forced by catastrophe. We stand today at a threshold eerily similar to those that once demanded reinvention from our ancestors: a world of accelerating climate volatility, swelling seas, and skies still littered with the remnants of cosmic artillery.

The essential question is no longer whether advanced knowledge existed before the Holocene, but whether we—armed with vastly more tools and awareness—will heed the warnings encoded in myth, stone, and sediment, or repeat the ancient pattern of forgetting. The choice before us is stark: memory or amnesia. And memory, as this book demonstrates, is far more than recollection; it is a survival strategy.

Lessons from the Shards of Forgotten Civilizations

From Göbekli Tepe's star-aligned pillars to the Piri Reis map's ice-free Antarctic coastline, anomalies pierce the official timeline like beams of light through a curtain. Taken alone, each fragment may invite skepticism; together, they form a chorus too resonant to ignore.

The lesson these fragments impart is twofold:

1. **Advanced knowledge once walked this Earth**, whether in the hands of a lost mother culture or in dispersed yet connected enclaves of genius.

2. **Civilizations are not immune to obliteration.** The Younger Dryas firestorm, the 536 CE volcanic shroud, and the countless local collapses remind us that progress is not guaranteed.

We have inherited not just tools and texts but warnings—some carved into stone, others sung in myth, and still others encoded in the isotopic rhythms of ice. To dismiss them as superstition is to gamble our future on arrogance.

The Cyclic Nature of Catastrophe

Across four continents, nanodiamonds, microspherules, and soot layers whisper the same refrain: cataclysm is cyclic. Every 1,450 years, every 2,980 years, every 11,600 years, Earth's record pulses with environmental resets. These are not random. They are the metronome of the cosmos, the drumbeat to which empires have unknowingly marched.

If the past is a pattern, then our era is no exception. We may not know the exact date of the next cosmic visitor or solar convulsion, but probability insists it will come. The question is whether we will enter that trial blind or prepared. Catastrophe, as the ancients seemed to know, is not the end but the terrain through which resilience is tested.

The Danger of the Comforting Myth

Civilizational amnesia is rarely accidental. As *Hidden Truths* explains, the "knowledge filter" operates both institutionally and psychologically. Inconvenient discoveries are dismissed not always through conspiracy but often through the subconscious defense of a progress narrative that insists: "We are the pinnacle. The past was primitive."

This myth is narcotic. It soothes us into complacency, discourages vigilance, and blinds us to the lessons encoded in both anomalies and catastrophes. But comfort, as history proves, is a dangerous indulgence. When the sky darkens, myths cannot feed a population, nor can denial shield a city from fire from above.

Building the Citadels of Knowledge

The path forward, then, is not simply to unearth the past but to prepare for the future with the humility our ancestors once carved into stone. Several imperatives emerge:

1. **Knowledge Arks:** From lunar repositories to high-altitude glyphs, we must encode survival wisdom beyond the reach of rising seas, political collapse, or digital decay.

2. **Transparent Archives:** Knowledge hoarded is knowledge lost. Open-source databases, mirrored globally, can democratize survival science.

3. **Resilient Infrastructure:** Food, energy, and data systems must be designed with dual epochs in mind—stable times and cataclysmic resets.

4. **Education for Continuity:** School curricula should treat catastrophe planning not as paranoia but as civic responsibility. Teaching children to read the sky, decode myths, and simulate resilience is no less important than teaching mathematics or literature.

These are not luxuries; they are necessities. We do not know when the next black layer will mark our epoch in the ice cores of the future, but we know it will come.

Humanity's Role in the Long Continuum

The veil, as this book argues, is not an impenetrable wall but a membrane. Press hard enough with questions, and it flexes, grows translucent, and finally tears—revealing not gods or monsters but our ancestors, beckoning us to remember. They are not relics but collaborators across time, passing the baton of survival.

Accepting that baton means renouncing the comfort of tidy timelines and embracing the responsibility of guardianship. We are not the culmination of history but one chapter in a story that stretches tens of thousands of years behind us and, if we choose wisely, tens of thousands ahead.

The Call to Action

The comet's wake will shine again. Whether it writes our obituary or our renaissance depends entirely on the decisions we make in the brief interlude of calm we call the present. The ancients encoded their warnings in monoliths, myths, and maps. Our task is to decode, preserve, and act upon them.

Thus, let us commit:

- To catalogue anomalies without prejudice.

- To build archives immune to both censorship and cataclysm.

- To train new generations not just in facts but in resilience.

- To honor the memory of those who endured before us by ensuring their lessons are not lost in the next fire or flood.

In the end, history is not a museum diorama behind velvet ropes—it is a living crime scene, its evidence surfacing piece by piece. The verdict remains unwritten. And the question is no longer *what did they know,* but *what we will do with what we now know.*

The veil has thinned. The trail grows stranger. The torch is in our hands.